Passionate Landscape
The Painting Journeys
of Buffalo Kaplinski

PASSIONATE LANDSCAPE

THE PAINTING JOURNEYS

OF

BUFFALO KAPLINSKI

BY

HARMON S. GRAVES

Foreword by
B. Byron Price, Director
Charles M. Russell Center for the Study of Art of the American West,
University of Oklahoma

SUNSTONE
PRESS
SANTA FE

Book design by Vicki Ahl

Sunstone books may be purchased for educational, business, or sales promotional use. For information please write: Special Markets Department, Sunstone Press, P.O. Box 2321, Santa Fe, New Mexico 87504-2321.

Library of Congress Cataloging-in-Publication Data:

Graves, Harmon S.
    Passionate landscape : the painting journeys of Buffalo Kaplinski / by Harmon S. Graves.
        p. cm.
    Includes bibliographical references and index.
    ISBN 0-86534-498-1 (hardbound : alk. paper)
    1. Kaplinski, Buffalo, 1943- 2. Landscape painters--United States--Biography. I. Kaplinski, Buffalo, 1943- II. Title. III. Title: Painting journeys of Buffalo Kaplinski.

ND237.K227G73 2006
759.13--dc22

2006014667

WWW.SUNSTONEPRESS.COM
SUNSTONE PRESS / POST OFFICE BOX 2321 / SANTA FE, NM 87504-2321 /USA
(505) 988-4418 / ORDERS ONLY (800) 243-5644 / FAX (505) 988-1025

CONTENTS

COLOR IMAGES LISTED BY PAGE NUMBER

PHOTOGRAPHS AND DRAWINGS LISTED BY PAGE NUMBER

Where Does It Start, Where Does It End,
plein-air watercolor, 11" x 30" 1996.
Collection of Steve "Grizzly" Adams.

FOREWORD

Chicago artists had been making the trek to New Mexico for aesthetic inspiration for several decades before 26-year-old Ronald Kaplinski, wheeled his Ford Mustang into the plaza at Taos in 1966. At least three members of the famed Taos Society of Artists had once called the Windy City home and two of that august group, Walter Ufer and E. Martin Hennings, had been prominent illustrators there. They, along with Victor Higgins, a talented young easel painter had traveled to the Land of Enchantment with the help of Chicago Mayor Carter H. Harrison Jr., meatpacker Oscar Mayer and several other well heeled patrons. Ron Kaplinski, who fled Illinois and the numbing pace of commercial art a half a century later, came west on his own hook, with only his hopes, dreams and God-given creativity to sustain him.

Although by the time Kaplinski arrived in the charming mountain community, the Taos Founders and the organization they had brought into being had long since passed into history, their artistic legacy lived on. The color, light, diverse cultures and monumental vistas that drew painters to New Mexico like a magnet were still in evidence as well. Yet American art and the country itself had undergone profound changes in the intervening decades. The Great Depression had caused widespread economic and social dislocation in the 1930s and the Second World War had ushered in the Nuclear Age making the world a far more dangerous place. By the 1960s, divisive issues of race, class and gender dominated the nation's political, economic and cultural landscape.

In the world of art, Abstract Expressionism had replaced Depression-era Regionalism and Social Realism as the dominant American art movement of the 1950s. The following decade saw Andy Warhol and Roy Lichtenstein unleash a Pop Art juggernaut that signaled yet another shift in public taste.

Ron Kaplinski, whose look and demeanor soon earned him the sobriquet, "Buffalo", yearned to be a full-time painter of western America, though not in the narrative and detailed representational tradition of such past masters as Frederic Remington and Thomas Moran. Wisely, Kaplinski followed his own artistic muse. Emotion ruled his palette and the individuality, spontaneity and improvisation that characterized both his work and his life saw him through false starts and lean years that would have discouraged a less committed artist. In 1967, he moved to Colorado, where his color-saturated vision of the natural and made-made landscape began to arouse the interest of galleries and collectors. There he joined other free spirits who dreamed and depicted a different West.

As footloose as a cowboy, Kaplinski's desire to travel and catholic taste for the world's wonders often carried him far from home though never very far from a compelling scene to sketch or paint. Committed to truth but never conventional, Buffalo Kaplinski's work embodies a spiritual dimension that describes the artist himself—open, transcendent and powerful.

B. Byron Price, Director
Charles M. Russell Center for the Study of Art of the American West, University of Oklahoma

Kayenta Prayer, **acrylic on canvas, 60" x 60" 1983. Collection of Mr. and Mrs. Harmon S. Graves**

ACKNOWLEDGMENTS

As I followed the course of Kaplinski's career, acknowledging what new challenges in subject matter and technique he undertook without fear of alienating his collectors, I wondered whether others really supported his freedom to interpret and desire to avoid predictability.

From time to time I'd encounter Rosie Stewart at Kaplinski's shows and we'd dance around the issue always finding something to praise in his new work, yet not willing to fully embrace each change of palette and subject.

Rosie has been an ardent collector of Kaplinski's work and as a docent at the Denver Art Museum and later the President of the museum's Volunteer Council, she had become an articulate critic of a wide range of contemporary and classical art. Her judgment is sound.

When Kaplinski's paintings of Greece were first shown—a remarkable transition from the soft earth tones of the Southwest—she and I clearly sensed that he could draw the best from whatever surroundings in which he chose to immerse himself, and that his style and technique would expand with his worldwide sense of place. It was then that the first thoughts of this book developed. Rosie had the first look at an early draft of my manuscript and authorized my use of her corruption of a phrase from "Home on the Range" ("Where Buffalo Roams") which earned preliminary consideration as a possible title of this book. I am indebted for her encouragement and wit.

Jerry Ravenscroft, a perceptive dealer in Estes Park, Colorado who handled Kaplinski's work in the 1980s, emphasized that to effectively promote the artist and his work he needed to observe in the field how Kaplinski chose his scenes and wrestled them onto paper and canvas. This, of course, led me to undertake the same analysis.

I am grateful for the permission granted by Edsel & Eleanor Ford House to reproduce Cézanne's beautiful painting, *La Montagne Sainte-Victoire*, for the unrestricted access to Burnham Hoyt's notes and construction drawings for the Red Rocks Amphitheater granted to me by the Denver Public Library, and for consent granted by The Mattatuck Museum to reproduce Frederic Church's *Icebergs*. I thank Marco Alvarez for the use of his whimsical cartoon which I entitled in this book *Curious Observer*.

Many thanks go to my daughter Jessica and my wife Nada for constructive manuscript review for the sharing of some robust laughter over some vignettes concerning our mutual friend, Buffalo Kaplinski. To Elizabeth Cunningham of Joseph, Oregon (formerly of Taos, New Mexico), whose editing talents and encouragement led to the publication of this work, I owe the gratitude of every author to a talented and persistent editor.

Earl August Hauck, a fellow lawyer and collector of many of the "Seven From Denver" artists' work thoughtfully shared anecdotes of these colorful characters—many of which were best told over lunch and a drink rather than in the pages of this book.

And to those who provided their impressions, insights, and gossip through which the reader, unfamiliar with the artist, can grasp a sense of his character and wit, I thank Vicky Kaplinski, George Carlson, Len Chmiel, Bill Sharer, Ned Jacob, Sandra Wilson, Jon Zahourek, Kay Wisnia, Phil Panum and Sally Schrup.

Finally, to my talented and long-time friend, Buffalo Kaplinski, I owe a greater understanding of art and nature, and of the far reaches of the world where he has been and someday I will go.

PROLOGUE: MAY IT PLEASE THE COURT

The day started out well. Rose-gold light glinted through the treetops. On a crisp late-winter morning, the sun began to warm roadside patches of ice. Upslope stands of Ponderosa pines lay deep in snow while wafts of moist mountain air promised spring. Taking the back road from Evergreen to Georgetown, Colorado, we had time to enjoy the drive and outline testimony to be presented in Clear Creek County Court.

I looked at my client. He was sporting a moustache and beard, wearing a baseball cap, and dressed for the chores he was performing when I picked him up—cleaning his art studio of the residuals of inspirations that never made it to paper or canvas. I had a sense that this was not going to be a routine petition for change of name. "Buffalo," a sobriquet laid on him by one of his artist pals, Ned Jacob, years ago when he was hanging out in Taos looking like a cross between Buffalo Bill and General Custer, was no slouch when called upon—heck, any opportunity was enough—to comment on his work, or art in general.

Curious Observer. Cartoon by Marco Alvarez, Mexico 1990.

We pulled up to the white clapboard courthouse on Argentine Street in Georgetown and sloshed through the usual mixture of mud and snow. As we entered the building, a glance at the court's Monday morning docket suggested that this could be a long session. Among the docket entries were half-a-dozen DUIs, a few domestic violence charges, and a bunch of disorderly conduct matters. There we were at the bottom: "In the Matter of Ronald Robert Kaplinski, Petition for Change of Name."

"All rise," the bailiff directed. The judge assumed his position on the bench and requested us all to be seated. We watched with heightened expectation as his eyes moved through the long list of matters before him, and settled on the last entry.

"Let's hear the Kaplinski Matter." A muffled groan rumbled among the People's defendants. I could understand that—they had been locked up over the weekend and only wanted out. One could hear the unexpressed pleas, "Charge me, let me go home!"

We approached the bench. The Court, with perspicacity, remarked, "Kaplinski'—I can understand why you might want that changed. Proceed counselor."

"No, your Honor, it's his first and middle names we seek to change," I responded.

"What's wrong with 'Ronald Robert'?" the judge remarked with a hint of sarcasm, not expecting an answer, only inviting the presentation of evidence.

So I began. "May it please the court" (a relic by which the advocate does not expect to invoke the pleasure of the court with regard to the matter before it, but if counsel has the slightest hope that the judge will pay attention to what is to follow he'd better begin with that), "I call Mr. Kaplinski and request that he be sworn."

"Please state your name," I inquired.

"Ronald Robert Kaplinski," he responded with his hat, thankfully, in his hand, speaking directly to the judge.

"What are the reasons for seeking to change your first and middle names?" I continued.

Without hesitation he replied, "I'm a fine artist and I have signed several hundred paintings 'Buffalo Kaplinski,' a name I have used ever since Ned Jacob hollered at me across the Taos Plaza in 1967."

"What is a 'fine artist'?" I asked.

No sooner had these words left my lips I recognized that we were in for an earful. Although a transcript is not available, his poignant soliloquy, recalled here as best memory will permit, provides a starting point for a study of this remarkable man and his art.

He began.

"Fine art is art concerned with the creation of beautiful objects that stimulate emotion in the artist and the observer. If it fails to spark emotion, it flunks as a work of art. I saw some of the best in the Chicago Art Institute, as a kid walking from gallery to gallery, and I knew even at that point what drew me to a painting."

"The more labored works of the nineteenth century were remarkable in their structure, capture of light, and subject matter, but it was those works which demonstrated solid drawing and unabashed use of light, particularly the plein-air artists toward the end of that century that encouraged me to do what I do. The effects of outdoor light couldn't be observed in a studio. The artists had to go where the light was—outdoors."

"Irving Shapiro, the late watercolorist, influenced my approach to drawing, tonal value, and solid technique. Roy Mason's work encouraged me to work on the spot, directly from nature. Some of my best work has been created from a campstool or the tailgate of my truck, interrupted only by a strong wind, rain, snow, a stray mountain lion, or cloud cover which altered the scene too much or risked what had been already placed on paper."

He forged on, disputing the narrow sense of place with which some artists say they are content. He had found inspiring material throughout the United States, Central and South America, including Mexico, Guatemala, Ecuador, and Peru. Quite a travelogue he gave.

Kaplinski paused. The pendulum on the old Regulator clock continued its suddenly loud methodic beat. Fifteen minutes had gone by.

"Where do you show your work?" the judge inquired, obviously caught up in the discourse.

"Odette's Gallery, a few blocks away from here, carries a few of my pieces."

"Well counselor," turning to me, "unless you have some evidence that the change of name would be detrimental to the interests of any other person, the petition will be granted."

With that, several hundred paintings were legitimatized, and over the three decades which have since passed, Buffalo Kaplinski's work has done what he told the court fine art must do: capture emotions and convey the artist's interaction with a specific place. The pages that follow show how the place both imposes on the artist the requirement to capture its individuality, and dictates how he paints in response to it.

THE ARTIST'S SENSE OF PLACE

I n *A Sense of Place: The Artist and the American Landscape*, Alan Gussow writes about "the qualities in certain natural places which certain men and women have responded to with love." The certain men and women he speaks of are artists, who through their paintings, left "a record of their encounters with the land for others to see, read and understand." Further, to look at the huge canvases of the great nineteenth-century American artists Thomas Moran, Frederic Church and Albert Bierstadt, is to feel the wonder of places like Yellowstone and Yosemite, the Andes and the Arctic, when these places were discovered and interpreted by such skilled painters, and brought before the American public for the first time.[2]

For all of us have loved places; all of us have laid claim to parts of the earth; and all of us, whether we know it or not, are in some measure the products of our sense of place.

—Alan Gussow[1]

This same sense of wonder and discovery is evident in the work of Buffalo Kaplinski. On a recent painting and camping trip to Lake San Cristobal near Lake City, he discovered a waterfall while hiking the Colorado backcountry. The thought occurred to him, while capturing the play of water as it descended granite rocks, that he was possibly the only artist who had ever painted this particular place.

In common with several nineteenth-century American artists, Kaplinski finds a mystic kind of beauty in nature. As he becomes familiar with a place, a subject grabs him, seduces him; he, in turn, interacts with the subject. Maybe it's the color of the rocks, or the way the light hits them, or the configuration of the geology. In these he senses deep mystery. As he discovers areas that are indescribable, he feels he can't possibly paint them. Then the challenge arises. "Can I do it? Can I aspire to interpreting the scene?" Reflecting on these dynamics, Kaplinski realizes that's what makes painting so exciting. "The strength of the artist is constant development. By repeating that which comes easily, perhaps as innocent as a pleasing composition, my work would lose its emotional excitement.

Kaplinski at Machu Picchu, Peru 1968.

What the heck," Kaplinski adds, "that's not even fun! By traveling and dealing with unfamiliar material I'm required to stretch—paint differently, and use a different combination of colors."

Other artists had different opinions about traveling to unfamiliar places. Georges Michel, who has been described as the forerunner of the Barbizon School, restricted his artistic horizons to the outskirts of Paris. "The man who cannot paint for a lifetime within an area of ten miles is just a clumsy fool who is searching for mandragora and will find nothing but emptiness."[3] Michel is not alone in this assessment. Picasso in one of his rare comments about art observed: "I believe it must be very annoying to go to the other side of the world—as Matisse did, following the route of Gauguin—in order to end up with the discovery that the quality of light and the essential elements of the landscape which the eye of the painter perceives, are not so different, after all, from those he would find on the Marne or the Ampurdan." [4]

"Ah," but Kaplinski rejoins, "an artist must stretch or stagnate. New places force new techniques and color to honestly interpret the landscape. An artist could, of course, and I think many do, tackle a new scene in a predictable way using a scheme he has used before because it is easy. I *want* the challenge!"

All three views have a common nexus: the land or sea and the sky above it. And it matters little whether it is pristine or altered by man; it is the place itself—the sight, sound, and smell of it—that provokes a need in the artist to record or interpret.

Like Frederic Church, who traveled in the mid-1800s in quest of exotic landscapes in the Andes, the Arctic, and the Middle East, Kaplinski succumbed to the allure of the unfamiliar. As he is fond of quoting: "The eye never has enough of seeing." He was forever seeking out new territories to test his artistic abilities. His initial trips to South America whetted a wanderlust that would take him to faraway places. After a thorough, fifteen-year investigation of what the Americas had to offer, Kaplinski traveled to other continents. He found foreign travel equally exciting. "There's something mystical about going to a place I've never seen. I don't know what will happen, what I will encounter. There's beauty all around us, but in a foreign country I get to see unique places and interact with different peoples. I'm exposed to their language, their food and other aspects of their culture." These trips stimulate his growth as an artist. Each trip is a catalyst for changes in his style of working, and has resulted in increasingly complex paintings.

Often attracted by natural wonders, national parks or wilderness areas, Kaplinski also finds lands steeped in ancient history compelling. Often a magazine article or a television travelogue will spike his interest in a particular country or region. Before setting off on a major painting trip, he researches the people and places he intends to visit. He reads travel brochures, scans books and catalogs, and gleans information from the Internet.

Packing for a painting trip requires one additional bag—the one of consequence—containing paints, pencils, brushes, palette, paper, drawing board, and, yes—a camera. "The amount of luggage I need is actually preposterous. Certain art supplies needed are virtually impossible to get overseas. If I only did sketches it would cut down a lot, but since I do completed paintings, that's a different story. Every time I leave I ask myself if I'm nuts to take all this along. I envy the traveler who can get by with a backpack and a toothbrush."

Everywhere he travels, Kaplinski carries sketchbooks with him. He steeps himself in the atmosphere of the place, then makes sketches as mnemonic devices to use the next day or next week to be able to recall every detail. Then, once back home, he musters his feelings and recollections and creates a larger, finished studio piece. Although he carries a camera, Kaplinski is no snap-shot artist whose sketchbook consists of a set of photographic prints, the source of studio renditions for scenes not committed to memory. More often than not, Kaplinski's camera records the artist at work rather than the work of the artist. [5]

Kaplinski's travels to Alaska, Latin America and later to Greece, the Middle East, Spain, Morocco, England, and other parts of the world, forced him to expand, adjust and experiment with his color selection. Inspired by his extensive travels and new horizons, Kaplinski recognized the need to tune his table of colors to new surroundings. At the beginning of his career, the subdued palette learned from Irving Shapiro, his Chicago mentor and instructor, lent itself nicely to traditional Midwest motifs, and in that setting, adopted in substantial part by Kaplinski, it worked well. When he moved west to Taos, New Mexico, and later to Denver, Kaplinski recognized that minimal obedience to the brilliance of the western sky and earth tones commanded the use of yellows, permanent green, raw sienna, cadmium orange and a variety of reds and blues. Even his renowned "monochromatics" are faithful to the light and colors of the Southwest—providing impressions of its prairies and canyons that slip effortlessly into the mind's eye. In his travels to foreign lands, the warm palette with which he became so comfortable in the Southwest surrendered, perhaps most dramatically, to crisp contrasts of the blues of the Mediterranean Sea reflecting the white plasters of Turkish mosques and Byzantine domes of the Greek Isles.

"A lot of people have accused me of going overboard on the colors," Kaplinski laments. "But I feel that my paintings are very honest in the colors. I try to go for the pure colors. If you look at a sunset, for instance, or shadows at different times, there's a tremendous amount of variation. Some people see gray shadows all the time. Lots of artists do. But I see violets and blues and all kinds of things in there."[6] Kaplinski believes, as did the Impressionists, that shadows are more appropriately depicted in blue tones, and that pure black almost never exists in nature. [7]

Kaplinski, indeed, saturates his paintings with light and color, but no criticism has yet been leveled that the passionate and feverish intensity with which they are applied are not a successful evocation of place. That, after all, has been his goal, and given the dominating influences encountered along the way, he was destined to achieve it through plein-air techniques applied extravagantly throughout many parts of the world.

Pierre Bonnard, the French Post-Impressionist painter, saw color much the same way. Quite unexpectedly, and on a rare visit to the Denver Art Museum, Kaplinski paused before Bonnard's 1913 *Dining Room in the Country*, a colorful indoor scene that takes the viewer to a garden beyond.

"Look," he exclaimed, "the door, tablecloth, and cat are white, but painted with violet and blues. And he wasn't afraid to use electric pink—even lemon yellow—on other items to show how the outdoor light affects the colors of the room!"

Their common sense of extraordinary color went beyond these two artists' depictions on paper and canvas. Bonnard cut a familiar figure in Paris with his 1911 yellow Renault, at a time when Henry Ford condemned all cars from his production line to black, while unknowingly yielding the distinction of the most colorful to Kaplinski's 1957 pink Chevy. This vehicle was Kaplinski's bright-hued ferriage from a successful, but uninspired, career in Chicago to Taos, New Mexico where his fine arts career began.

CHAPTER 2   CHICAGO: THE FORMATIVE YEARS

" I haven't used Payne's gray since I left Chicago and headed west in 1966," Kaplinski was quick to observe. The somber shades of the city's landscape and the conservative palette of his mentors at the American Academy of Art were perhaps the fuel that fired his love of light and color that surfaced in his paintings in later years.

Born in Chicago in 1943, Kaplinski received some of his early art instruction in the city's public school system. His parents, Genevieve and Jacob, were both working folks—his mother holding down a night shift job at Maurice Lennel's cookie factory and his father on the day shift as a tool and die maker at McCormick Works for International Harvester—so the budding young artist's penchant for drawing was first detected by Gertrude, a baby-sitter who cared for him and his brother Jim. "Ron," known by his given name at the time, "will draw anything," Gertrude happily observed. Perhaps she found the care of this youngster easier if pencil and paper were provided.

Kaplinski offering early work at Street Fair, Chicago ca. 1964.

By age eight he had begun making "stream of consciousness" drawings with crayolas. In response to the budding artist's talent, his family provided him with his first studio—a former coal bin in his grandfather's basement at 2715 North Ridgeway Avenue. "It was cleaned up, painted, and I had my own

Grandfather's Basement, **watercolor, 12 ¾" x 9 ¾" 1962. Collection of the artist.**

private world!" [1] One of his earliest surviving paintings, *Grandfather's Basement*, reflects Kaplinski's early ability and already keen powers of observation.

Kaplinski's introduction to plein-air painting occurred at an early age. On one of the family outings to the Lake Michigan shore, the youngster shyly approached a young woman, working in watercolor, skillfully reproducing the rip-rapped shoreline with its pounding, wind-driven water and blue-gray sky. He was fascinated with the immediacy of it—a scene being faithfully created with such ease as he watched. Kaplinski recalls his mother asking the artist how she acquired her skills. Her reply was straightforward: "A good teacher and lots of practice." This was to be Buffalo's guiding principle.

Kaplinski's training began under the attentive eye of Hildagard Melin, a pastor's widow, who provided Saturday oil painting lessons at her home in Chicago—75¢ for group sessions and $1.25 for a private lesson. Mrs. Melin preferred instructing in oils, and provided her young aspirants with solid composition and color techniques. As was typical at the time, her students laboriously copied reproductions of master works. Kaplinski's efforts to reproduce one of Thomas Moran's Grand Canyon scenes did not challenge the rightful place of Moran as a master painter of the grandest of all landscapes, but it is interesting that he selected a Southwest scene to copy. That region would so dominate his early professional works that he was initially known as a painter of the Southwest.

Kaplinski began his formal training in 1954 at age eleven at the Art Institute of Chicago. On the weekend his mother would make the fifty-mile round trip by bus with her son so he could attend the children's Saturday art classes held at the museum. There the teachers encouraged their pupils to experiment as they worked with paint and clay and learned design techniques. After classes he was free to roam through the Art Institute's collection, where he saw some of the finest paintings in the world. He feasted his eyes on pictures by famous American artists like James McNeill Whistler, Winslow Homer, and Mary Cassatt. He also admired the lyrical works of nineteenth-century French landscape painters.

An exhibition of John Singer Sargent's work at the Art Institute, which Kaplinski toured with his mother, made a lasting impression on the budding artist. The exhibit included Sargent's watercolors demonstrating his plein-air style. These were clear favorites. It is not just the synergy between the young artist and his admiration of the works of an acclaimed contemporary painter that warrants comment. What seems remarkable is that Mrs. Kaplinski, lacking any exposure to the arts, whose dual role had always been a co-provider and mother with little time and resources for cultural experiences, recognized the need to expose her son to an exhibit of this kind. He still recalls his mother's upbeat invitation to this exhibit: "Come on, Ron." she said, "We're going downtown on the bus to see something important!"

In addition to his early studies at the Art Institute of Chicago, Kaplinski recalled the excellent art instruction he received in the Chicago public schools. However, like generations of artists before him, his greatest education came from viewing masterpieces at the Art Institute. "I'd spend hour after hour looking at the achievements of the greats, and I'd constantly be thinking, Look at all these techniques. Each one is so different!" [2]

After high school and his studies in fundamentals and design at the Art Institute of Chicago, Kaplinski began studies at Chicago's American Academy of Art located on the corner of Adams and Wabash. In the course of the two-year program, he increased his artistic skills and his familiarity with tools and techniques in the school's commercial art classes. Kaplinski was especially taken by the watercolor class, and blossomed under the tutelage of Irving Shapiro, watercolorist and master teacher. Shapiro taught a fundamental art class, and an advanced class for watercolor students. Kaplinski participated in both, and credited his teacher with the lasting skills he acquired in drawing, tonal value and technique. One recollection from his student days extols the respect Kaplinski held for Shapiro: "Irving was serious about his instruction, articulate, and very specific in explaining his painting theory. We were silent and pretty much in awe when he demonstrated. He would present a short lecture as he effortlessly illustrated his points. He was the true master of the No. 8 round red sable brush. Very direct and clean washes were his forte."

Maxwell Street on a Rainy Day – Chicago, **watercolor, 8 ½"x 22 ½" 1964. Collection of the artist.**

Railroad Yards – South Side, plein-air watercolor, 13" x 26" 1963. Collection of the artist.

Shapiro was part performer too. One mannerism remains vivid in Kaplinski's mind: "After making an important statement about theory or technique, Irv would raise the rim of his eyeglasses just a bit and then let it drop as if to punctuate his words. "Got it?"

From Shapiro, Kaplinski acquired the essentials of transparency in watercolor—working from light to dark, using a wash to suspend particles and allowing the richness of a Fabriano paper to show through. His considerable influence surfaces in much of Kaplinski's early work.

Searching for new material, Kaplinski's adventures often took him to Maxwell Street on Chicago's Southside. Newly arrived immigrants found not only work and shelter, friends and family in the Maxwell Street neighborhood, but also a gateway to the culture and life of Chicago and, on a broader scale, the way of life in the United States. Maxwell Street's significance goes beyond its repute as a port of entry: it is also known as the birthplace of the "Chicago Blues," launching such luminaries as Bo Diddley, Muddy Waters, Howlin' Wolf and Paul Butterfield.

Three Stacks, Chicago, plein–air watercolor, 13" x 26" 1963. Collection of the artist.

As he wandered through the market area, Kaplinski experienced Maxwell Street's cultural and musical heritage. Street vendors hawked fruit from barrows; plucked chickens hung in the storefront windows. The aroma of baking bread yielded intermittently to the sweet scent of boiling red cabbage, and whiffs of Chicago hotdogs, smoked fish and redolent garlic. He encountered a cacophony of blues horns, boom boxes and electric guitars. A melange of Europeans, Puerto Ricans, Jews, and Blacks, in various garb, working or idling, enjoyed the familiar sounds and smells of their neighborhood. With all senses turned on high, Kaplinski drank in the colorful figures in every doorway and on the street corners. Not far away, the stockyards, steel mills, warehouses, and back alleys of the produce district provided challenges for architectural themes, constructed with more somber, but rich colors.

In these early Chicago cityscapes it is as if his apprenticeship were one of composition, form and darkness. He uses shape and monumentality combined with deep dark shadows, cool blues, greens, saturated yellows and reds to capture the blurry gray asphalt, pitted and weathered brown factories or abandoned buildings dirty with decay. Kaplinski's darker palette shows both the influence of his teacher, Irving Shapiro, and that of the city. His handling of the Chicago railway yards, docks and warehouses is direct.

He does not lecture the viewer about the way man-made structures have too often violated the landscape, but instead captures the beauty in the arrangements of tracks, stacks, girders, and drab buildings coaxed into additional years of service or left to stand hollow-eyed.

While these paintings are successful, they have little of the looseness and intense color that would awaken later in his paintings in the high desert country of the American Southwest, for which he has been so highly praised.

Kaplinski landed his first job in 1962 at Chicago's Barry Nolan Studio as an art apprentice in advertising design. A year later Anderson Studio hired him, first as an apprentice, and some months later put him "on the board" to work with clients. This early experience made a lasting impression on the young artist's work: to this day Kaplinski credits the strong sense of design in his work to the time he spent working in advertising art. His jobs in commercial art and illustration provided him with an abundance of art materials and unlimited time after hours to experiment with them. [3]

A commercial art studio had another benefit, according to Kaplinski. He found his fellow artists to be good and thoughtful people who liked to share ideas and philosophies. As an art apprentice, he observed seasoned illustrators and graphic designers at work. Kaplinski questioned them about technique and use of materials, "and so I was able to get firsthand instruction from topflight people." His boss, Stan Anderson, himself a watercolorist, encouraged creativity and experimentation in the workplace—an additional bonus. [4]

Lou Heiser, an illustrator with whom Kaplinski worked at Anderson Studio, added other elements to Kaplinski's technical armamentarium. He advised Kaplinski to be patient, but persistent. Heiser said that a good artist must have accumulated sufficient "brush mileage." Translated, this meant years of experimentation and interpretation, and proper handling of the brush. The artist learned to time the application of water and pigment so as to seduce the viewer's eye to accept, for example, the depiction of distance and depth. While these are by no means revolutionary concepts, under Heiser's periodic tutelage Kaplinski's skill and confidence quickly grew. Heiser detected that and bought several of Kaplinski's paintings, making him one of Kaplinski's earliest patrons.

Recognition of Kaplinski's talent and growth followed within a year when Anderson Studio promoted him to art director. George Carlson, who worked with Kaplinski as an illustrator, remembered Kaplinski pointing to two bottles lining the shelves of his office labeled "Talent" and "Inspiration." Tongue-in-cheek, Kaplinski would exclaim, "Those are my sources."

While the artists often played jokes on each other, Carlson recalled Buffalo's intensity when he worked: he would often do twenty washes on 20 x 30 inch illustration board to get one that he liked. [5] Carlson couldn't resist. He created a convincing version of one of the best of Kaplinski's studies, placed it on the floor behind Kaplinski at work, stood on it and tapped the artist's shoulder with the familiar "How's it going?" Then with a horrified look towards his feet Carlson exclaimed, "Jeez, Ron, I'm sorry. I didn't see it!" Kaplinski, stunned for a second, looked with horror at his study-gone-door mat, but Carlson's broad smile belied this apparent disaster. Kaplinski didn't take the bait. These two pushed each other hard, and as we shall later see, their friendship was again tested among the cottonwoods and intense New Mexico sky.

Kaplinski continued to experiment with various water media: gouache, acrylic, traditional watercolor, casein, gesso, alone and in combination. Often he would scrub into the wet surface of the painting with crumpled paper towels or score into an area with razor blades to add texture. Water media gave him freedom and fluidity, creating rhythm. While he worked quickly, passionately, his movements almost frantic, the eye and hand working together, he none-theless had control of his brush. Unlike traditional oil paint, water paints cannot be corrected, so the artist must commit to the brush, the pigment, and the movement of the hand. Kaplinski came to know ahead of time how all of these elements would act in concert. Paintings built upon themselves as he stepped into a timeless state, seeing the beginning and the end with a simultaneity.

The deftness and surety of his painting, his loading the brush knowing just how much pigment the brush carries, and his attacking an area with consummate skill, can be felt by the viewer. The negative spaces, the shapes—some hard edged, some softly moving into one another—with the underlying abstract composition, became elements that would set him apart. The strongly colored areas bouncing against each other and the immediacy of his vision, which had its beginnings in Chicago, are what later made him unique among contemporary landscape painters. [6]

Kaplinski's job as art director at Anderson Studio came to an abrupt halt after he asked for a raise. Stan Anderson refused it. Kaplinski quit Chicago, heading west in his pink '57 Chevy. After driving from Oklahoma through Tucumcari, New Mexico, he arrived in Santa Fe. On Palace Avenue he noticed that the Shop of the Rainbow Man was showing watercolors by his idol at the time, Roy Mason, and oils by Ross Stefan. Kaplinski showed his work to the owners, Hal and Gwen Windus. They agreed to carry some of his watercolors. Kaplinski drove on to Taos, then Ouray, Colorado, and ended up in Denver, where he collapsed in love with the woman who managed the boarding house where he had a room. The love affair and dreams of being in the West ended abruptly when his hands were scalded and blistered while washing dishes in a restaurant on Colorado Boulevard. Some good news, however, arrived just before he returned home—the Shop of the Rainbow Man had sold four of Kaplinski's watercolors for $25.00 each. Back in Chicago, he worked briefly for Diamond International designing egg cartons, and for King Korn Stamps—the Chicago version of S & H Green Stamps. The only gentile among the Jewish employees, Kaplinski was treated with great kindness. When his art director announced a Christmas party! Kaplinski joined the group at Mr. Kelly's to hear a comedian who would later rise to stardom—Woody Allen.

In 1965 Kaplinski advanced his career when he went to work as a graphic designer for Handelan Pedersen, a prestigious Chicago advertising firm. Handelan had captured a narrow niche in commercial advertising: shoe illustrations. Kaplinski was told that his lettering had to improve. He took a class to master this technical requirement, but still found this aspect of illustrating to be monotonous. He grew increasingly dissatisfied with the commercial art world. Creativity was missing. When Kaplinski announced he was quitting, the art director said: "You'll be back." Kaplinski retorted: "Not a chance!" To his mother's chagrin, he decided to be a painter. Encouraged by his small sale at the Shop of the Rainbow Man, he would soon test his capacity as a fine artist in Taos, New Mexico. [7]

CHAPTER 3

TAOS: BARBIZON OF THE SOUTHWEST

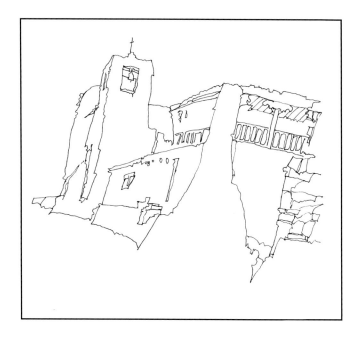

Church at Acoma. **Drawing by Buffalo Kaplinski**

In 1966 Kaplinski packed his art supplies in his new racing green Ford Mustang, left Chicago and headed west. Taos was not new to him: he had stopped there, then moved on to Denver in 1964. Before that he had driven from Chicago through Taos and other parts of the West when he contracted to deliver a rental agency car to Phoenix in the early 1960s. What struck him then and has stuck with him was that Taos offered a potpourri of Spanish and Pueblo culture, sculptural adobe buildings, big skies, and dazzling light—a sharp contrast to the somber tones of urban life in Chicago.

Roughly fifty years prior to Kaplinski's arrival in Taos, Walter Ufer, one of the early Taos artists and member of the Taos Society of Artists, posed a reasonable hypothesis: "Who can say that the Santa Fe-Taos School of Art may not in the near future mean to American art what the Barbizon School has meant to France?" [1] Like the French nature painters of the mid-to-late-nineteenth century, the early Taos artists were driven to find places to paint landscapes away from the drabness of industrialized urban life. The French painters found inspiration in their coveted Forest of Fontainebleau forty-five miles from Paris; the Taos artists found it in the pueblo-dotted landscapes, with their colorful native inhabitants, and in the nearby mountains, valleys, and canyons bathed in the brilliant New Mexico sunlight.

Ufer may have been a bit expansive in his optimism about the impact of the Santa Fe-Taos art colonies on American art. Since the 1920s, however, Taos and Santa Fe have attracted competent artists who still have available to them a good part of the subject matter which the early Taos and Santa Fe artists enjoyed. Like their French counterparts, American painters moved away from the industrial and urban environment of the city to be in a place where they could step out of their studios, and paint *en plein air* (in the open air) directly from nature.

The early Taos painters found a landscape of vast cactus-and sage-covered mesas; deep canyons carved by the Rio Grande; red sandstone arroyos cut by wind and water; and huge forested areas in the mountains—all within a few miles of the village. And so it is not surprising that Kaplinski and a cadre of companions, who recognized the importance of light, color, varied landscapes and the striking native Pueblo and Hispanic people, headed south in the footsteps of Taos art colony founders, Bert Phillips and Ernest Blumenschein.

Echoing the history of the early painters who formed the Taos Society of Artists in 1915, some of Kaplinski's contemporaries had become residents by the time he came on the scene in 1966. Ned Jacob arrived in Taos in the early 1960s, and Bettina Steinke, an established local artist with a gallery connection, quickly recognized his talent and provided needed encouragement as well as a meal or two. William E. (Bill) Sharer soon followed.

Kaplinski had met Sharer in his student days at the American Academy of Art in Chicago, when Sharer was operating the Academy's art store. Kaplinski considered him "one of the most unfriendly SOBs I had the displeasure to meet." Sharer's stint as a Marine drill instructor just prior to his art studies in Chicago may have compromised his civility. Nevertheless, Kaplinski's first impression faded away a few years later in Taos when he encountered a different

William Sharer, *Kaplinski,* **oil on board, 15½" x 10½", Taos, N.M. 1967.**

Sharer—this one polite, courteous, and easy to be around. Kaplinski recalled "Willy" as being "a quiet and introspective guy, who never had anything bad to say about anyone." Sharer had a mongrel dog, his constant companion, named Whitey that everyone loved. When he wasn't busy painting, he would pack up Whitey in his old VW bus and go fishing. Seemingly never separated, Kaplinski and his cohorts used to joke that Willy would be buried in the old bus—dog, fishing gear, and all. Later on, when Sharer moved to Santa Fe, he let the visiting Kaplinski stay in his studio. Despite Kaplinski's early Chicago impressions, the two became good friends. [2]

For the record, Sharer and Jacob were both responsible for the Buffalo moniker. In describing Kaplinski to Jacob, before the two even met, Sharer maintained that with his long hair, waxed mustache and goatee, he looked like Buffalo Bill. After meeting Kaplinski, Jacob began calling him "Buffalo" Kaplinski, alternating it with "Winslow" Kaplinski (for one of Kaplinski's early artist heroes, Winslow Homer). "You have to admit 'Winslow Kaplinski' had a ring to it," says Jacob "but 'Buffalo' finally won out." [3]

Not long after Kaplinski found a place in Taos, George Carlson hooked up with him and worked a deal to share the adobe studio, once occupied by Taos modernist artist Clay Spohn, overlooking a sheep meadow on Valverde Street. [4] Carlson had worked with Kaplinski at Anderson Studio, and like Kaplinski, he yearned to abandon commercial art for a career in sculpture. He sought to jump-start the transition in Taos.

The two were unlikely companions. Their approach to art making differed. The more philosophical Carlson would do in-depth research before tackling his subject. In Taos first he studied the mythology, stories, and dances of the Pueblo people, and then began to work from a live model. Carlson likened his own approach to an old campfire smoldering under dry moss, which when fanned by the wind, burst into flames; whereas Kaplinski was intense, a man already on fire. He would set up, and boom! paintings would literally erupt from his brushes. Ned Jacob had another observation from personal experience: any painter working near Kaplinski risked being coated with a flurry of paint splatters. [5] Their creative efforts rarely clashed—Carlson sculpting from Indian models he recruited from the Taos Pueblo, and Kaplinski experimenting with an ever-brightening palette of colors. The conflict arose after work hours. Carlson found relaxation in reading the great philosophers while Kaplinski needed a good dose of rock and roll. The sound of rock may have spoiled the serenity of philosophical thinking.

Carlson's reminiscences paint a picture of their time in Taos. The two young artists got by on little—cooking massive amounts of pinto beans, with the occasional tripe, bacon, a little meat, maybe some lettuce. "We lived like monks," Carlson said. This simple life allowed Carlson and Kaplinski artistic freedom: they no longer had to bend to the whims of commercialism. In Taos there were no distractions, no looming deadlines, no demanding art directors. The two had the luxury of spending most of their time devoted solely to living and making art. They could live cheaply in a community long acquainted with and tolerant of artists; they arrived in Taos at a time when Leon Gaspard, one of the early Taos artists, was still living, and where they had easy access to the works of such venerated Taos painters as Ernest Blumenschein and Victor Higgins.

All four artists suffered a slender livelihood in Taos. Kaplinski remembered Bill Sharer being able to live on $500 a year; Ned Jacob would parcel out a pound of hot dogs, eating two a day, in addition to a slim ration of bacon and eggs. [6] His sense of humor intact, even in hard times, Kaplinski often said: "Art is like that . . . one day you eat chicken, the next day you feast on the feathers." [7] Yet these financial hard times were worth it to each one of them—they could devote themselves entirely to their art. Kaplinski recalled that for the first time in his life, he had the opportunity in Taos to "eat, sleep and live art." Art became his foremost thought: he lived only "to create art, to paint, to go outside to look for new subjects to paint."

There was no scarcity of artistic subject matter in Taos and its environs, but food and other necessities demanded a more intense pursuit. In Taos the centuries-old barter system was still active and credit was available to creative types. In these lean times, the young artists helped each other out. When one of the group sold a painting, he would help the others buy food or treat them to a meal. Ned Jacob ran up some pretty hefty bar tabs between painting sales and was generous in allowing the others to add to them. Kaplinski had a trade-out deal worked with Brad's Pizzaria, but Jacob didn't draw against it, being a little suspicious of some of Brad's pizza toppings.

The unparalleled master of barter, however, was Jon Zahourek. Art supplies, food and booze—three staples of Bohemian artists—were unabashedly exchanged for drawings and paintings. While Zahourek never took up residence in Taos, he regularly visited from Denver. He met Kaplinski through Sharer and Jacob. Zahourek recalled meeting his "Slavic soulmate" in the Valverde Street studio: "Buffalo was outrageous, a wild man. He wore black, pointy shoes, shiny Polish suits—the stylized equivalent of a Chicago zoot suit. He was a real diddy-bopper, listening to tail-dragging deep Chicago blues." With Howling Wolf and the Paul Butterfield Blues Band blasting in the background, Zahourek saw "killer paintings" on the studio walls, and immediately arranged a trade with Kaplinski. [8]

When Zahourek came to Taos on painting trips, his artist friends would put him up, and sometimes he would go on occasional painting excursions with them. In Denver he would reciprocate by hosting them whenever they came to visit. Zahourek, together with Kaplinski, Sharer, Jacob and Carlson, formed the nucleus of what later became known as the Denver-Taos Circle of Artists, an informal association of artists who worked and showed in these two communities in the late 1960s and early 1970s. [9]

With their camaraderie and support for each other this informal association of artists, who found their way to Taos in the 1960s, echoed what the Taos Society of Artists experienced at the beginning of the twentieth century. As Kaplinski put it so well, they were artists who liked each other and, most of all, had great respect for each other's work. "We would look at each other's work, possibly criticize it, and share information on collectors, galleries, dealers. Nobody really knows how tough it was." This sharing of resources on all levels helped them survive the lean years in Taos.

By this point in his career, Kaplinski was pretty well committed to plein-air painting. He had traced the steps of Leon Gaspard whose sable brush a half a century before had made Twining Canyon in the Sangre de Cristo range north of Taos a familiar scene for gallery goers in Santa Fe and as far east as Kansas City. The permanency of its granite blocks standing as proud survivors

Rio Grande Gorge, Taos, acrylic on canvas, 18" x 24" 2001. Private collection.

of cascading water from Taos Mountain contrasted sharply with the broken and twisted tree trunks wedged among them. Kaplinski energized this alpine study with colors that even Gaspard would not have dared to apply.

At the opposite extreme, the area's other prominent geological feature—the Rio Grande Gorge—attracted Kaplinski's brush just as it had that of Ernest Blumenschein years earlier. Located eleven miles northwest of Taos, this spectacular crack in the earth plunges to a depth of 650 feet below the Rio Grande Gorge Bridge. Like Blumenschein, Kaplinski had a fascination with the gorge and painted this subject repeatedly over a period of years. In a review of his work in *Taos News*, the artist stated what drew him to Taos: the stark contrasts in color and in tonal value as well as the "extreme geologic beauty" of the gorge and the surrounding mesas. [10]

His observations of this landscape, and the skills he acquired in painting it, would serve him well in later years when painted the canyon lands of Utah and Arizona.

Kaplinski also succumbed to the beauty and originality of one of Taos most famous man-made landmarks, Taos Pueblo. From the founding of the art colony in 1898, Taos Pueblo, its architecture unique in the United States, has attracted the brushes of painters. Built in the pre-hispanic period, sometime before 1400, and occupied continuously from that time, Taos Pueblo today is the largest surviving multi-storied Pueblo structure. Made from sun-dried mud-and-straw bricks, the five-stories of the Hlauuma (or North

Taos Window, watercolor, 7½" x 9½" 1970. Private collection.

House) seem to grow out of the earth. The forms of the building echo the silhouette of the mountain. When the sun sets on the adobe building, it glows cadmium yellow. This color phenomenon led Spanish explorers to believe they had located one of the fabled golden cities of Cibola.

Apart from architecture of the great canyons and the close-to-nature structures of the Pueblo Indians, Kaplinski found that some of the funky buildings of the Anglos and Hispanics of the region provided winsome material. His *Taos Window* documents some architectural expediencies of the local inhabitants. The descending rust marks on the tin roof, akin to water stains streaking down canyon walls, serve as a startling reminder that southwest contemporary cultures may be as transient as those of the earliest inhabitants of the neighboring canyons. Kaplinski's curiosity and early years spent painting the people and the architecture of Chicago's Southside now translated into something deeper in his painting of the ancient cultures and architecture of the Southwest. His fascination with these subjects would continue throughout his painting career.

The environs of Taos and the nearby villages also had their allure. Arroyo Hondo, the inspirational haunt of Taos artists for decades, beckoned Kaplinski too. Its patchwork of plowed fields bordered with cottonwoods tucked between its timeworn hillsides, was the usual mien sought by these Taoseños. Arroyo Hondo's cemetery, however, presented a *mise en scène* of crosses, *santos*, flowers, and memorabilia of the departed framed by a weatherworn fence. While rarely the entire focus of a painting, impressions of this scene would later find their way into Kaplinski's plein-air and studio works.

Often in the company of one or more of his fellow Taos artists, Kaplinski went further afield to find new subject matter. During an outing he made with Bill Sharer to Tesuque Pueblo and Abiquiu, Sharer recalled them joking around and having a good time, but when they stood side-by-side and started to paint, they got down to serious business. [11] Kaplinski's more frequent painting pal, George Carlson, spoke of one significant painting trip to Cabezón, New Mexico. The two artists planned to stay in the area for six to eight weeks and paint in the small villages nearby.

They had come equipped with all the camping and painting gear they would need for their lengthy excursion. While they were prepared for the elements—rainstorms, thunderstorms, and other perilous challenges nature might provide—they were not prepared for a dangerous human encounter. Both artists had a deep respect for the Pueblo and Hispanic people, and were

The artist with local children, Abiquiu, N.M. 1969.

careful not to camp on anyone's private land. One night, they had a surprise visit at two a.m. from several angry Hispanic men in a pickup, yelling: "Get off our land, you damn gringos!" Knowing that Kaplinski had a short fuse, Carlson crawled out of the tent, and explained that they thought they were on land owned by the Bureau of Land Management; and out of respect they would be glad to leave, but only when they could see well enough to strike their tent and gather their camping gear. The men told them they had to be gone by 6 a.m. By the time the men in the pickup returned, Carlson and Kaplinski had struck the tent and packed up their supplies. When the men, now more sober, discovered that the two gringos were artists, they asked if they could paint signs that read "PRIVATE PROPERTY NO TRESPASSING." Carlson quickly agreed that they were the men for the job—they had both done hand lettering in a Chicago advertising firm. Not only were they happy to oblige, but they would also paint the signs for free. They made a few signs the men could post with elegant lettering—converting the harsh message to words of beauty. They parted as friends, the men giving the two artists directions to a nearby ranch on the Rio Puerco owned by Joe Chavez.

When Carlson and Kaplinski introduced themselves to Chavez, on recommendation from some of his neighbors who thought he might allow two artists who respected and loved nature to paint somewhere on his spread, Chavez obliged. He pointed out a place where they could camp near some ironwood trees, telling them they could stay as long as they wanted to. For the rest of their stay, Chavez would invite Carlson and Kaplinski to the ranch house for dinner, or would visit them at their campsite. Not only did the artists come away with sketches and plein-air paintings from that trip, they developed a warm friendship that lasted until some years later when Chavez died in the course of a cattle drive. [12]

Back in the studio, Kaplinski took the most appealing designs and re-inforced them with his own personal viewpoint—never a literal translation of the landscape. His plein-air work became so immediate, so dynamic, that he knew ahead of time what technique would produce the effect he was working toward. His results were gaining acceptance. In 1966 when he showed with thirty-nine other resident Taos artists at the Stables Gallery, a critic comment-

Sky of The Kachinas, watercolor, 24" x 40" 1967. Collection of Mr. and Mrs. Bruce Vanderberg.

ed on his work: "Kaplinski is especially delightful in the freshness and subtle flavor of place which he brings to nearly abstract descriptions of the Pueblos in his monochromatic watercolors." [13]

Blair Gallery in Santa Fe sponsored a solo show of Jacob's drawings in 1967 and this loose association of artists rallied around one of their own—and perhaps more closely around the wine and tidbits, the usual gallery chum. Typical of the group's mutual support, Jacob soon convinced Don Blair to take his fellow artists into the gallery. Blair gave Kaplinski a solo show in August 1967, and wrote about his work in the accompanying brochure: "Since coming to Taos Mr. Kaplinski has roamed over much of the Southwest recording it with a fresh eye and with a technique that is only Kaplinski. He often packs his painting equipment and climbs miles into the interiors of mountain and desert country to capture the dramatic quality of the landscape that has seldom been seen by city dwellers. His watercolors have a crisp and fresh quality not unlike nature itself." [14] In recognition of Kaplinski's talent, Blair honored him with a second solo show the following summer.

Sky of the Kachinas, shown at the 1967 Blair Gallery exhibition, is typical of the kind of painting Kaplinski was doing at the time. For scale he set tiny figures against ground or sky in juxtaposition to the landscape, to convey the

Cuatro Cruces, New Mexico, **watercolor, 15½" x 24" ca. 1971. Private collection.**

enormity of the Southwest's vast spaces. He chose a color that best expressed his emotional response to the place he was painting. To carry the sense of the emotion throughout the work, he used a limited palette or colors adjacent on the color wheel, to augment the original chosen color, a color that so dominated the painting that Kaplinski later dubbed them "monochromatics." His "*Cuatro Cruces, New Mexico,*" confines the viewer to another point on the color wheel while opening a wide vista in which imagination may roam.

By the summer of 1967 the interpretive skills of the modern Taos muse had been well recognized. Bill Sharer and Ned Jacob would periodically take forays from Taos to the various pueblos scattered along the Rio Grande to paint the inhabitants, their villages, and colorful ceremonies. Jon Zahourek, working out of Denver, but finding periodic inspiration in Taos, was addicted to the female form, and continued with that subject matter. Gradually Indians, their costumes, and dances became a significant addition to his portfolio.

The concept of the American Indian depicted through time, first by the Taos founders and then by those who followed in their footsteps, led to a remarkable exhibition that year at the New Mexico Museum of Fine Arts in

Santa Fe entitled *The Changing Image of the Indian*. Interpretations of the Indian and his surroundings by Kaplinski, Jacob, Sharer, and Zahourek challenged those of Taos Society of Artists members Ernest Blumenschein, Irving Couse, Walter Ufer, and Oscar Berninghaus. Yet the changing image was respectful. The moderns maintained their tie to the roots of their predecessors.

By now Kaplinski had a succession of gallery owners who had faith in him: Hal and Gwen Windus' Shop of the Rainbow Man was succeeded by Margaret Jamison of Jamison Gallery, and later Don Blair of Blair Gallery in Santa Fe; and Ivan Rosequist of Mission Gallery in Taos. His work had been included in a major museum show in Santa Fe. Yet, for all the acclaim, Kaplinski was barely scraping by in Taos. Ned Jacob urged him to move to Denver. Jon Zahourek suggested that he could bring a little color to the Colorado Institute of Art if he were inclined to teach. A steady although modest paycheck had its appeal. And so the smell of piñon burning in countless corner fireplaces, sunsets that stretched the full breadth of the horizon, dusty streets, rebozo-clad old Spanish women colorfully competing with the blanket-draped Indians from Taos Pueblo, were left behind as Kaplinski rode through the umbrella of cottonwoods shading Paseo Del Pueblo and headed north to Denver.

Steep Backyard. **Drawing by Buffalo Kaplinski.**

Kaplinski's arrival in Denver lacked fanfare. When asked what brought him to the Mile High City, he replied: "Starvation!" Jon Zahourek helped him find a job at the Colorado Institute of Art. Kaplinski worked there for a year, using his skills in commercial art to teach design and layout. Through his friendship with Zahourek and his job at the Colorado Institute of Art, he soon found his way into Denver's art world. Within six months, Kaplinski had found a collector and patron who believed in him: Aline Kaiser. She purchased two large watercolors in those early months, then advanced him the money for others to be sold through her gallery, Rive Gauche. In October she gave Kaplinski his first solo exhibition. Her brochure shows her understanding of the artist's work and how the Southwest had shaped it. Kaiser wrote about Kaplinski's "dynamic yet sensitive handling of space and color" which she felt was the soul of his work. She found in his paintings "the quiet dignity of the people who wander the land, the stark mesas that haunt the desert night, the entire panorama of life and the living. Bold ochres and fiery wastelands typify his landscape fulfilling the artist's theory of man being insignificant in relation to the power and scope of his environment." [1] The following spring, Kaiser sponsored a two-artist show for Kaplinski and another Taos transplant, George Carlson.

In 1968, a year after Kaplinski's move to Denver, he along with Sharer, Jacob and Carlson, received wider recognition when the Museum of Natural History hosted an exhibition of their work titled *Southwestern Artists*. Although they each had exhibited separately at other museums outside Colorado, this was the first museum exhibition in Denver to show them as a group.

By 1969 Ned Jacob had interested Steve Owen in his work. Owen was the proprietor of the Owen Gallery located in Larimer Square, an island of upscale boutiques, restaurants, offices, and galleries housed in newly restored relics of the 1800s. Owen had created an attractive gallery space in the Square, but was focusing on works of artists from the East Coast who lacked a reliable

Castle Rock and Pikes Peak, plein-air watercolor, 14" x 22" 1992. Collection of the artist.

following in Denver. Jacob's work, then largely devoted to American Indian genre paintings, was the obvious answer. When Jacob suggested that Owen consider work by a few of his peers and pals, Kaplinski, Carlson, Zahourek, and Sharer, he had little trouble convincing Owen to redirect his focus to the Southwest.

Of those early Denver days, Kaplinski recalled that "everyone's career was hanging by a thread. We were all struggling. When people are having a tough time, there's that camaraderie and bond for survival." One would have expected fierce competition for gallery sponsorship and Denver patrons among these artists. Yet none broke rank. The sharing of occasional windfalls from Taos days now grew into recommendations of each other's work to a growing number of collectors. What a rare camaraderie!

In the March 1969 exhibition, *Recent Works by Buffalo Kaplinski, Ramon Kelley, Ned Jacob, Bill Sharer*, Owen noted that Kaplinski had "a strong rapport with the outdoors which is evident in his powerful monochromatics. His object is to convey to the viewer, by using the fewest possible brush strokes, the omniscience . . . of the universal experience." [2] The works Kaplinski showed at the time grew out of watercolor studies he made of Monument Valley, Canyon

High Country Cow Camp, **acrylic on canvas, 20" x 24" 1978.**

de Chelly, and Mesa Verde. Kaplinski's work at this point in his career was summed up—by the artist himself and by critics—as "monochromatic." Despite the absence of a broad spectrum of color, the nuances of those he chose were faithful to the light and mood of the Southwest, providing impressions of its prairies and canyons that slip effortlessly into the mind's eye.

As he responded to other hues and compositions encountered in the course of his travels, a wider range of colors swirled on his palette—finding only a moment's refuge before applied to the new scene structured in pencil on the paper before him. Returning, as he would from time to time to scenes of the Southwest, Kaplinski revised his approach: minimal obedience to the brilliance of the western sky and earth tones commanded the use of yellows, permanent green, raw sienna, cadmium orange, and a variety of reds and blues.

Rocky Mountain Jigsaw Puzzle,
watercolor, 21" x 28" 1990.
Collection of the artist.

While patrons of Owen Gallery found consistency in the quality of Kaplinski's work, they never encountered predictability.

From their very first show this cadre of artists, who shared tough beginnings in Taos and then migrated to Denver, inspired a dedicated following of predominately young collectors who were willing to venture wherever the artists' works were displayed. Odette's Gallery, located in Georgetown, the nineteenth-century mining hamlet west of Denver, was one such destination.

Once again the gallery door was opened by one of the artists, and the others were soon invited. Wally and Odette Baehler, the proprietors of Odette's Gallery, made exhibitions of the paintings and sculpture of these artists festive events. They carefully culled and supplemented their list of invitees with the care of the most socially-minded hostess in Denver. Add to the chosen few, a coterie of cowboys and hangers-on from the Red Ram bar, and Kaplinski looking like—well, Kaplinski—and one had the characters of a Steinbeck novel.

Times were so good, a collector had to resist the temptation to step

Paul Cézanne, *La Montagne Sainte–Victoire,* oil on canvas, 65cm x 81cm, ca. 1904. © Edsel & Eleanor Ford House, Grosse Pointe Shores, Michigan.

to the bar after the sometimes challenging drive from Denver before taking at least a preliminary gander at what was hung on the walls. Red dots were posted quickly on the obvious favorite works, and others soon followed.

Wally Baehler had good gallery savvy. When he sensed that a collector was hesitating to open his wallet and simply needed a slight push to purchase a particular painting, Baehler would move in for the kill. Politely excusing himself while he snatched the painting from the view of a few of his patrons assembled around it, he and his recalcitrant client headed to a small room with an overstuffed chair facing one wall. The customer was doomed. He sank deeply into the comfort of his place of honor from which it was no easy task to rise—and no escape. Baehler would place the singular work under a gallery lamp which he could dim or brighten, all the while extolling the nuances of light which perhaps even the artist didn't know were there. Suddenly, now recognizing what he had missed in his original consideration of the work, the bedazzled customer was not about to lose the opportunity to purchase.

Relief from such gallery gimmickry came in painting trips Kaplinski made as he explored the Rocky Mountains of Colorado. His fascination with the nuances of rock formations has placed him in some good company. In the late 1800s French painter Paul Cézanne, who had used the same careful application of modulated color to enhance the formal qualities in his work, also devised a type of brushwork that helped him to emphasize structure in his paintings. [3] This technique comes to light in Cézanne's depiction of Mont Sainte-Victoire painted in 1904. The artist's response to the warm hues of the sunlit face and cool colors of the shaded north slope is subdued yet powerful.

Kaplinski's treatment of Mount Sneffles, near Ridgeway, Colorado, offers the viewer a similar architectural formation, yet with strikingly bolder colors. The results of both are harmonious. In Cézanne's painting, after patient observation, the viewer is gently seduced by the soft colors, while Kaplinski's palette commands attention, forcing the eye quickly through the yellow middle ground on to the cirque and ridges of the mountain. For the topologist, views of Montagne Sainte-Victoire from a slightly different angle present a very similar mountain profile to that captured by Kaplinski in Colorado. Topography, however, is not the common ground. Recognition of a magnificent scene, breathlessly awaiting interpretation, is what bonds landscape painters and transcends generations and styles.

By now Kaplinski had proven himself as a painter. He had established himself successfully with gallery dealers and collectors in New Mexico and Colorado. Inspired by his travels in the two states, he began to travel further afield. In his Taos days, he had shared adventures and a studio with George Carlson. Some months into their Taos adventure, Kaplinski's heartthrob from Chicago, Clarice Pinkola, announced that she too wanted to head west. Carlson was out, Clarice was in.

Kaplinski had met Clarice Pinkola in Chicago while both were working at the upscale advertising agency, Handelan-Pederson. One day as Kaplinski negotiated the shaky steps of the agency's circular staircase, headed for his stu-

Big Rock Candy Mountain, **watercolor, 13½" x 22" 1995. Collection of the artist.**

dio, he lost both his balance and control of his morning cup of coffee. The hot liquid cascaded onto Clarice, working at the company's reception desk below, splashing all over her and staining her new beige linen suit. In typical Kaplinski style, he offered up a gift-wrapped box in lieu of the dry cleaning bill. The box contained a Batman comic book, a Mickey Mouse watch, and a note that read "I'm very sorry. Can we be friends?" [4] Their friendship blossomed in Chicago, matured in Taos, and grew into marriage the spring of 1967 in Denver.

The couple's first years in Denver centered on survival as Kaplinski concentrated on his painting career and Clarice worked to promote his work. The year he spent teaching at the Colorado Institute of Art helped pay the bills, and supplied Kaplinski with art materials. The couple stayed with Jon Zahourek until they found an apartment in an old Victorian house at 1012 Pennsylvania Street in Denver's Capitol Hill area. The rent was so cheap that Kaplinski soon rented a small space in the same building to use as his studio. When he wasn't teaching, he directed his energies to painting. The couple's hard work paid off nearly a year later. They found a house at 4590 Grove Street in northwest Denver that suited their domestic needs, including in the huge backyard, a garden. A moat for irrigation divided plots into his and hers. The earth spoke to Kaplinski. Jon Zahourek recalled: "Buffalo's side looked like a jungle. Clarice's looked like the aftermath of the battle of Verdun." [5]

The Grove Street home became home base for their travels. The vigorous Clarice shared Kaplinski's wanderlust and sense of adventure. She accompanied him on painting trips all over New Mexico, Arizona, Utah and Colorado. Together they hiked miles in areas that they could access, and often hired Indian guides and packhorses to get to more inaccessible regions. They hiked the ruins at Chaco Canyon and at Canyon de Chelly. A Navajo guide took them to the Keetseel and the Betatakin cliffhouse ruins. Their dedication to exploring new frontiers eventually led them to Latin America.

CHAPTER **5**

LATIN AMERICA: MAYAN RELICS, MARIPOSAS, AND MOONLIGHT IN MACHU PICCHU

In the late fall of 1968, not long after Kaplinski married Clarice Pinkola, the two set out to explore Mexico. The landscape of the Southwest and the cultures of the Pueblo, Hopi and Navajo people had fascinated them both. After painting trips to the Southwest, the promise of new horizons with the colorful cultures and the beautiful crafts just over the border lured them further south. A visit to one of the border towns on his initial trip to the Southwest had piqued Kaplinski's interest. In preparation for their trip, he recalled them both reading up on Mexico, and Clarice reading the journals of Bernal Días del Castillo, one of Cortés' soldiers. They planned to drive from Denver to El Paso, then on to Mexico City.

Here were two gringos determined to teach each other Spanish en route as they drove through the arid landscapes of Colorado, New Mexico, and Texas. After crossing the border, they soon learned that a vocabulary error made by one not only went uncorrected, but was reinforced by the other. *Habla*, Spanish for "speak," suggests, by its initial letter, sound and length, that it must be the Spanish equivalent of "have," and so blank stares met their request for water with *Habla usted aqua?"*

The Kaplinskis' three-month tour of Mexico began in Nogales and continued along the west coast through Mazatlan, Alamos, the fishing village of San Blas, the seaport of Manzanillo and on to Patzcuaro. They stopped in Tzintzantzun, once the capital of a Tarascan Empire near Lake Patzcuaro, which is known today for its crafts. Kaplinski, however, was captivated by some of the architecture. He created a painting of a twin-gabled adobe house. Years later when he returned to Tzintzantzun on a trip with his son-in-law, Juan

The Sun Altar, Machu Picchu, Peru.
Drawing by Buffalo Kaplinski.

Dimas, Kaplinski wondered if the house was still standing. He found it, but his interest was drawn to another nearby—an art deco house surrounded by bougainvillea in full bloom. He set up to paint it. Then his concentration drifted as he heard the slowing pace of a passerby behind him—the moment plein-air artists dread. The footsteps came to a stop, the inevitable question suspended in interminable time. This time Buffalo was in for a pleasant surprise: no questions, only an offer to share a cold beer or two upon finishing his painting. Kaplinski's new-found acquaintance, Arturo, the house's owner, was himself an artist and understood well that no repechage is granted to the watercolorist—he must do it right the first time.

From Patzcuaro the Kaplinskis drove on to Mexico City. Despite their immersion in Spanish and the culture and history of Mexico, the two adventurers were unprepared for its immensity. From its inception the city has always served as the metropolitan center of Mexico. The city was originally known as Tenochtitlan, the ancient Aztec capital built in the mid-1300s. When the Spanish, under Hernan Cortés, arrived nearly two centuries later, they found to their astonishment a city of over a million in population. In a letter to the King of Spain, Cortés described Tenochtitlan's immense towers, high walls, beautiful buildings and huge temples. Terraced gardens and canals surrounded the city. The aqueduct that supplied the built-up island with water caused the Spanish to call it "The Venice of the New World." In 1521 Cortés overthrew the Aztecs, razed Tenochtitlan, and on top of its ruins built Mexico City.

When Kaplinskis arrived, the population of Mexico City alone had swelled tenfold since the arrival of Cortes. The ruins of the Aztec Templo Mayor had not yet been unearthed, and Spanish Colonial structures, like the cathedral and National Palace on the Plaza de la Constitucion, Mexico City's central plaza, dominated the core of the Old City. These cultural monuments were not enough to induce Kaplinski to open pad and paints; the bustle of *la gente* was simply too distracting. Sightseeing eventually gave way to Clarice's interest in textiles, and the couple soon headed to Puebla, then Oaxaca, where they found the distinctive cuisine, weavings and other handicrafts typical of the two regions.

With so much new subject matter to choose from, Kaplinski often opted to paint the architectural forms and street life he saw. Mexico's tidy plazas,

Arturo's Bougainvillea Casa, plein-air watercolor, 13 ½" x 17 ½" 1981. Collection of Jean Chrest.

el centro, the heart of every town, draw admiring tourists, yet present such predictability that the artist usually shuns them for unique streets and alleys nearby. Kaplinski was not deterred. Taking Pierre Bonnard's approach to the depiction of his garden in southern France, Kaplinski emphasized the rounded shapes of natural elements—the palm trees and sculpted gardens splashed here and there with crimson bougainvillea—while reserving straight lines for man-made structures. [1] The ubiquitous plaza was artfully released from its confinement to postcards.

Within months of their return to Denver, the adventuresome duo decided to make a second trip to Latin America. Drawn by stories of Guatemala, they loaded their Willys Jeepster with art supplies, a folder full of maps, a Spanish dictionary, clothes, food and other provisions and headed south. The Pan American highway was to serve as their link from Mexico through Guatemala, El Salvador, Honduras, Nicaragua, Costa Rica, and on to Panama City.

From there they would travel by air to Ecuador and Peru. The avowed object was to search for new flora, architecture, peoples and circumstances—the stuff of creativity. Kaplinski would later recall the challenges he faced as an artist: "Painting on the spot was the ultimate for me during our 1200 mile trip to the interior. Although there were certain handicaps; a savage heat, asphyxiating dust and wandering herds of mangy-looking cattle, the pleasure of having the actual subject matter before me nullified the disadvantages." [2]

Kaplinski recalled other challenging moments that could have put him and Clarice in real danger. Nicaragua and El Salvador were embroiled in a border war at the time, and border crossings anywhere in Latin America could be tricky. Crossing into Guatemala, Kaplinski recalled a border guard saying, "I'll get these papers signed for you, but are you my friend?" He replied, "Sure." Then the *guardia* said, "Well, my friend will help me with some money." Friendship, it seemed, was measured by the amount of the bribe! Paying this extra tribute irked Kaplinski. However, thinking back on the adventure, the border war, and the fact that he had hidden a pistol in the body of the Jeepster, Kaplinski shudders to think what would happen if he made that same trip today. "It's totally insane, nuts. Nobody in their right mind would do that."

From Mexico the Kaplinski's Latin American adventure continued through Guatemala where little conical harvest houses dotted the fields; El Salvador whose Spanish-style buildings were reminiscent of those found in the southwestern United States; Honduras, with its Mayan relics; Nicaragua with its lakes and volcanoes challenging the beauty of two coast lines and the seas beyond them; Costa Rica—the motherland of rain forests and colorful butterflies; and Panama where the bustle and unsightliness, in Kaplinski's view, of Panama City contrasts sharply with its pastoral outskirts. They were thrown headlong into this cacophony of cultures, colors and sounds, and emerged with a plethora of on-the-spot paintings, sketches for studio pieces, and sights committed to camera and memory for later expression.

From the trip through Central America, Kaplinski remembered Chichicastenango as one of the highlights. A two-and-a-half hour drive from Guatemala City, it is one of the places where modern Mayan people bring goods to barter and sell. Buyers and sellers from all over the area arrive for market day in this

Night of Santo Tomas, Chichicastenango, Guatemala, watercolor, 14" x 23" 1969.

highland town. Twice a week the plaza turns into a bustling marketplace where Maya-Quiché vendors sell their hand-woven textiles and other fine handicrafts. As Clarice inspected the beautiful modern Mayan textiles, the swell of sounds, the colorful garb of the Maya-Quiché people, and the odors of their food wares must have reminded Kaplinski of his hometown's Maxwell Street.

The church of Santo Tomas, located on one side of the plaza, becomes the focal point for fiestas, particularly at Christmas time. The Kaplinskis witnessed a Christmas Eve procession of the Society Confradía, where the people wore Indian garb and walked around the church with Christian icons. In the manner of people at Taos Pueblo, the modern Mayan people had developed a form of Catholicism steeped in their own ancient rituals.

After the procession had retired to the interior of the freshly whitewashed church, Kaplinski sat down cross-legged on the broad pavement, calmed by the gentle peal of the church bells and soft light. Luminaries dotted the way and led the faithful to the simple church door. He effortlessly created a series of sketches, but due to the absence of light, had to return to his room at the Pension Quigola to work on the painting. The muted joy of that evening is quietly reflected in the painting which he entitled *Night of Santo Tomas, Chichicastenango, Guatemala.*

After arranging to store the Jeepster in Panama City for a few weeks, Kaplinski and Clarice flew to Ecuador. Kaplinski never anticipated that the warmer orange-burnt sienna hues of the Arizona canyon lands would be encountered on this trip. Venturing into the drought-stricken highlands they witnessed the sun's merciless baking of the landscape and the body and soul of its inhabitants. This place had none of the joy of the canyon lands, where earth, sun, and sky have been prepared by nature to exist in harmony. Withered grass and leafless trees, yawning cracks in dried lake bottoms, and farmers' despair were the devastating response to nature's fickleness. Kaplinski created a few forceful plein-air watercolors, mournful in their creation and moody in their presentation, yet honest interpretations of this harsh landscape.

In Peru their destination was Cuzco, nestled in a broad valley of the Andes situated at 11,207 feet. Here they found a city with some houses made of adobe, open markets, and narrow, winding cobblestone streets—and a history similar to Mexico City. Known for its baroque churches and Spanish colonial architecture, *Cuzco,* like Mexico City, is built on the foundations of previous cultures. The Spanish conquistador, Francisco Pizarro, conquered the Incan capital in 1533, and rebuilt Spanish Cuzco in 1534. The name "Cuzco" comes from the Quechau word *qosqo,* meaning navel of the earth. Built in the fourteenth century, at its height Qosqo served as the capital for the Sapa Inca, a succession of powerful Incan rulers beginning in the mid-1300s, whose political stature equaled the pharoahs of Egypt. By 1470 Inca territory covered Peru and reached across the borders into Ecuador and Chile. Like other Inca cities, Qosqo had buildings and fortresses made of enormous ashlars, or hewn stone blocks, so perfectly fitted that they required no mortar.

The Kaplinskis adapted to these historical surroundings with the help of some maté de coca, a coca leaf tea, served at the insistence of their solicitous hotel staff to compensate for the lack of oxygen. They didn't linger long over the residue in their teacups and soon immersed themselves in Cuzco's colorful market place, the best place to see the descendants of the Incas. Native vendors displayed weavings and other high quality crafts, including the Inca "calendar" rug woven from the wool of sheep and alpaca. While Clarice bartered for textiles, Kaplinski crafted sketches of the market scenes. The

**Cuzco's Colonail Cathedral, Peru.
Kaplinski at work from a roof top.**

constant movement challenged his brushes; with so much activity he found it difficult to capture the scene. He relied on sketches and did some watercolors, then developed paintings back home in the studio, using the sketches and photos done in Cuzco.

Away from the bustle of the Cuzco market Kaplinski set up his easel on a rooftop close to a church basking in the late afternoon sun. His plein-air treatment infuses an earthy authenticity in his interpretation of this tranquil scene.

Due to the ruggedness of the Andes, there are few roads, so from Cuzco the Kaplinskis took a plane, then a train, and finally a bus to Machu Picchu. Upon walking through the Sun Gate, the ancient entrance to Machu Picchu, they were astounded. The journals of Bernal Días del Castillo, describing Mexico, fit perfectly the sight that greeted them in Peru, as they had their first glimpse of a place "never seen or dreamed of before." [3] They gazed in wonder at the ruins of the only entirely-intact and preserved ancient Inca city. Located 2000 feet above the Urubamba River and huddled in between the pinnacles of an Andean massif, Machu Picchu appeared to grow out of the surrounding rocks. To get a better look at the high walls, giant stone temples and fortress buildings, ramps, and *andenes* or agricultural terraces, they climbed another 1000 feet to Huayna Picchu, the peak above Machu Picchu. Kaplinski recalled the difficulty of hiking at that altitude, and that Clarice had to take extra care: in December 1969 a doctor in Costa Rica had confirmed her pregnancy and told her to take it easy for the rest of the trip.

To interpret Machu Picchu, the lost city of the Incas, and the lush rain forests waiting to envelope it, Kaplinski relied extensively on icy green blues and grays. One evening the plateau at Machu Picchu was framed by the rocky pinnacles surrounding it, with the Andean moonlight articulating the details of the ancient walls and foundations bathed in nocturnal aquamarine tones. Kaplinski absorbed the details of this tranquil landscape reserving it for a studio night scene—one of the few he has created.

Although still high from their visit to Machu Picchu, the Kaplinskis began to long for home. They flew back to Panama City, where Clarice, who had developed severe morning sickness and had been advised not to travel Panama's rough roads, took a plane to Costa Rica. She would wait for her husband to arrive in San Jose and they would drive back from there to Denver. In the in-terim, while Clarice rested and recovered, Kaplinski stopped for a week in the San Blas archipelago north of Panama. He stayed a few nights on a boat. During the day, Cuna Indians would arrive in their guide boats. These skilled navigators—descendents of Panama's original inhabitants who had traded pre-dominately by canoe along the Caribbean coast—ferried Kaplinski to outly-ing islands to paint. At the time he liked his gin and tonics, and invited his Cuna guides to join him. When he communicated his need for ice for the drink, he was surprised when one of the Cuna men showed up with some. In a tropical area with no electricity, he couldn't imagine where they'd found ice. The Indians' playful protestations of magical powers were exposed upon Kaplinski's discovery of a footnote in one of his guidebooks mentioning pro-pane refrigerators.

Iglesia de Cuzco, Peru, **plein-air acrylic on board, 15½" x 11½" 1968.**

Once back in Denver, Owen Gallery opened a major exhibit of Kaplinski's Latin American paintings. The gallery's March 1971 brochure denotes the changes the trip had wrought on the artist's work: "It's a Kaplinski of another mood entirely than the monochromatic studies of the Navajo Country of Arizona, a show of contrasts reflecting a long and thoughtful trek down through Central America and into Peru and Ecuador." [4] Given the artistic quality, it should have been no surprise that the show was well received. Kaplinski had captured the essence of life in Latin America in his paintings for the show. *Denver Post* commented on his "aerial views of rivers and jungles with networks of streams emptying into a huge river." The reviewer wrote that the artist's beautiful shades of green in one of his jungle paintings "reminds one of looking at life under a microscope." [5] Importantly, the exhibition demonstrated to Kaplinski that one's sense of place can be as broad as the artist may elect. The patron is not necessarily looking for a replica of where he has been, but maybe where he would like to be—even for a moment—through the eyes of the artist.

Two major family events followed on the swell of the exhibition's success. With a new house under construction, a third family member would soon move into the household's new location in Evergreen, Colorado. Awaiting the birth of their child, the Kaplinskis were convinced that the baby would be a boy, and if so, then he would probably be named Tovar, for *tovarish*, a Polish word meaning "friend." On September 20, 1970, the couple came up with a name for their baby girl: Tiaja, after a mountain range in his ancestral Poland.

In 1972, after the family moved into their home in Upper Bear Creek Canyon in Evergreen, Colorado, Kaplinski made another life decision. He changed his given name to Buffalo in 1973, a sobriquet hung on him by Ned Jacob during his early days in Taos and legalized many paintings that bore that signature.

Kaplinski at Machu Picchu.

Lone Fisherman – Panama City, Panama,
acrylic/watercolor on board, 11"x 24"
1971. Collection of Earl Hauck.

Clarice continued to promote her husband's work while seeing Tiaja through the toddler stage. In 1973, in response to Kaplinski's growing dissatisfaction with outside gallery representation, Clarice opened Phoenix Gallery. She worked as the gallery's proclaimed "proprietrix" until its closing in 1975. She had accompanied Kaplinski on many painting trips and knew his work and the places he painted intimately. A photographer and poet, Clarice was able to sense and capture the mood in Kaplinski's paintings through her poems. Her incisive verse tugged gently at the viewer's emotions, as in this poem that accompanied *Peyote Priest Vision.*

> We shook the harp of the wind, balancing
> on the slivered staves of desert shadow.
> We kissed the eye of the fire and shared
> red dust with the night scorpion. Suns
> scent woke us with crackled breaths. Our
> footfalls were eider echoless. Midnight
> sage cried a magic musk; cold moons called
> to the coyotes wife. Great chiefs tethered
> their hearts to Orion as White men lost
> fortnights in wagon ruts, and tore our
> absinthe moon from her spire.

Peyote Priest Vision, acrylic, watercolor and ink, 18" x 26" 1973. Collection of Camile Cazzedeus.

Another major event brought additional recognition to Kaplinski's work—and a new challenge. In 1971 Johns-Manville Corporation had acquired the 10,000-acre Ken-Caryl Ranch southwest of Denver as a site for its international headquarters. Prior to its use as a stage stop in the 1860s, then for breeding cattle beginning in 1914, the Plains Indians had used the land as hunting grounds. Legend has it that Colorow, Chief of the Utes, planned his attacks on wagons running from the Leadville mines on their way to Denver from a cave well-hidden by surrounding rocks and piñon trees. Adding to the history and grandeur of this place, spectacular sunsets, accentuating the huge red rock outcroppings, have for centuries played out their final moments to the mournful yowls of coyotes.

In order to create an aesthetic record of the ranch, Johns-Manville invited artists to provide their interpretations of the landscape, or its current or historical inhabitants. That decision grew out of a vision that Johns-Manville's art director, Philomena "Fil" Giuliano, had. She wanted painters and photographers to document this special place before the path of progress cut into the tranquility. To accomplish this, she and the corporation's publicist, Rosemarie Stewart, decided to choose local artists in the ascendancy of their careers. After soliciting suggestions from the Denver arts community, they selected thirteen artists, among them Kaplinski, George Carlson, Ned Jacob, Jon Zahourek, and Len Chmiel. The artists had full freedom of expression. The only criterion set before them was to depict some aspect of the ranch, that together they capture its essence. The artists responded with paintings and photos of Ken Caryl's flora, fauna, geology, architecture and ranch personnel. [6]

Rosie Stewart later recalled how Kaplinski's name kept coming up. He had a reputation as a young, outstanding landscape painter; one, she was assured, who could communicate the beauty of this big ranch nestled in the foothills. She remembered how getting to know all the artists "was a particular joy . . . Buffalo captured our eyes with his work our hearts with his conscientious dedication to the project and his unique personality." [7]

Kaplinski was already familiar with the area. George Carlson, in his search for eagles to sculpt, had discovered an aerie on the ranch land, and invited Kaplinski to join him on painting forays that crossed the "NO TRESPASSING" zone. After receiving the commission, fellow artist Len Chmiel joined Kaplinski on several painting rambles as the two sought inspiration for their brushes.

Given artistic freedom, Kaplinski spent the next three months making sketches and small plein-air paintings. One spot in particular drew his attention: a rock formation called Eagle Rock, a nesting spot for golden eagles. He painted several watercolors of Eagle Rock and others looking down into the valley to the plains below. The result of Kaplinski's effort, ten on-the-spot paintings and three studio paintings, became part of Manville's Ken-Caryl Heritage Collection.

The Kaplinski work selected for publication in the Johns-Manville catalogue, *A Heritage*, was a small, abstract plein-air watercolor employing rich greens and browns, depicting a view of the ranch's vast prairie grasslands as viewed from craggy mountain outcroppings above them. This was a substantial departure from his well-recognized orange, red, yellow, and purple limited palette treatment of southwestern landscapes. The catalog text, written by

Rosie Stewart in 1975, indicates Johns-Manville's satisfaction with Kaplinski's commissioned work: "This extraordinary landscape artist deals primarily with the awesomeness of nature."

Another commission, this one in 1975 through O'Grady Galleries in Chicago, became part of the Chicago Tribune's Bicentennial art collection. Kaplinski's painting of covered wagons on the Santa Fe Trail was part of a traveling exhibition that toured the country in 1976. From the artist's standpoint these commissions meant more than recognition and corporate sponsorship: they saw him through some tough times. But more was to come—his marriage to Clarice had begun to fray and the two divorced in 1975.

THE RANCH: RENOVATING A HOMESTEAD AND REKINDLING THE ARTIST'S LIFE

As his marriage deteriorated and he went through divorce proceedings, Kaplinski suffered in other ways. He had lost his gallery representation: Phoenix Gallery closed, and he had a falling out with Wally Baehler and finally severed ties with the Baehlers' gallery in 1975. He lost his home in Evergreen and didn't know where he would live. In his time of need, he turned to the circle of artist friends who had helped sustain him through other tough times.

George Carlson, whom Clarice had displaced as a roommate back in the Taos days, now lived in Elizabeth, Colorado, a one-hour drive from Denver. When Carlson heard of the pending divorce, he figured his old friend would need somewhere to live and told him about a place that was up for sale. Not sure he could afford it, Kaplinski decided to take a look anyhow. As he drove through the ponderosa-dotted landscape, he came to a shallow draw. On high plains near Elizabeth, it would provide modest protection from fierce prairie winds. At the end of the dusty road, he came to a group of run-down, weathered buildings including a magnificent log barn, gray with age. He later found out that the ranch, built in the 1890s, had once been a historic stage stop. Kaplinski purchased the ranch in 1975.

Alone and lonely Kaplinski looked at the prospect of reassembling his

The Kaplinskis' ranch house, Elizabeth, Colorado.

The Kaplinskis' 1890s barn, Elizabeth, Colorado.

life and remodeling his house, unaware that the Johns-Manville commission would soon bring another bonus: Vicky Smith. In 1972 she had met Kaplinski at the Little Bear Café in Evergreen, Colorado. Her mental note was short—a married man with a child was not a good romantic candidate. One year later, however, Kaplinski was producing a portfolio of material for the Johns-Manville Corporation's documentation of the Ken Caryl Ranch landscape before development. Sometime in 1975, Ed Morrison, the photographer preparing the inventory of paintings created for the Johns-Manville Collection and long-time pal of Vicky's father, had come to dinner at the Smiths' home. Conversation turned to the Johns-Manville project. One artist, in Morrison's view, stood out. He described Kaplinski, his work, and his single status. There was really no mistaking the man and his work, and his single status sparked Vicky's interest. She would find a way to renew their earlier acquaintanceship.

He had no telephone, the Internet didn't exist yet, and so contacting a hermit had to be done by mail. Her letter to Kaplinski at his recently acquired 1890s vintage ranch in Elizabeth, Colorado found its mark and after courtship and a cleanup of the ranch, Vicky and Kaplinski were married on October 18, 1976. Of the twenty-nine years of marriage that followed, Kaplinski observed:

"She has put up with a lot including projects remodeling the ranch in various phases. She's a good helper and art critic as well! She's probably the only person who understands me completely and has always been there for me."

With the contentment and base of support that Vicky and the ranch provided, Kaplinski returned to painting with a renewed vigor. In a review of a show that opened months after he married Vicky, the critic noted "beautiful and unusual works" saturated with color, some of them opaque, but all treated with a "transparent overlay that made them seem to glow from within." The reviewer found all works "meticulously executed and presented, displaying the self-assurance of an artist who is experienced with his media and subject matter." [1]

Veering off Kaplinski, the article devoted the rest of the space to Sandra Wilson and her alluring gallery on 1756 Broadway. While working for Don Blair, first in Taos, then in Santa Fe, Wilson had met and represented Kaplinski, Ned Jacob, Bill Sharer, and Jon Zahourek. After opening and managing her own gallery in Santa Fe, she transferred Sandra Wilson Galleries to Denver in March 1974. By that time all four artists had also relocated to Denver and were pleased to find representation with a gallery director so fiercely devoted to them.

By the time Wilson opened her Denver gallery, the artists she represented had reached professional maturity. [2] Her belief in "the boys" prompted her to promote their work outside the Denver art market. Recognizing that they needed national exposure at this juncture in their careers, she placed ads in *Art News*, *American Artist*, *Southwest Art*, and even the old *Apollo Magazine*, based out of London, England. Bill Sharer called Wilson and her gallery "the one biggest help to all the artists she represented." [3] Kaplinski, who considered

Kaplinski ca. 1977, Elizabeth, Colorado.

Little Coyote Ranch, acrylic/watercolor on board, 11 ½" x 27 ½" 1988. Collection of Mr. and Mrs. Harmon S. Graves.

her gallery one of the best he ever dealt with, echoed the group's feelings for Wilson: "From day one she was very professional. She never did anything on a shoestring. I think she really loved the artists and the paintings that they did." Len Chmiel spoke of her as a real supporter. "She pulled together this group of highly motivated artists. A mutual support system developed that has not been duplicated since. We were all very lucky." [4]

Reciprocally, the group's devotion to excellence, their attention to the traditional painting criteria, such as color, design and balance, generated the quality of work Wilson could believe in and promote. "All the artists were extremely concerned about using the best materials they could, about using their talents including knowing how to work with paint, brushes, canvas, paper, so they were engendering or fostering lasting art work." Wilson often felt like the den mother as her artists would come and go, sometimes to discuss their concerns, sometimes meeting in groups at the gallery to talk art. She recalled disagreements and differing opinions as they exchanged ideas. Since art making is such a solitary exercise, she felt these discussions kept the artists from getting tunnel vision—a way to both spur them on while simultaneously providing a reality check.

What struck Wilson the most about the group, however, was their mutual support of each other's work. "There was such a camaraderie. I've seen it to a lesser degree in other friends and acquaintances, artists that were in a circle of friends, but this group of guys would just as soon talk about another person's work as their own." When she visited a particular artist, it always amazed her to find more work in his studio by the other guys than by the artist himself. "That wouldn't happen in the East," she said.

From the Taos years, Wilson remembered Kaplinski's delight at being in New Mexico. "When he moved away from Chicago, he really came alive." After representing Kaplinski and showing the gamut of his works from various painting trips, Wilson was repeatedly impressed with the joy Kaplinski found in painting and his unbridled enthusiasm. That was something she felt stuck with people after they'd met him, that something which drew collectors to his paintings. "His enthusiasm, you can see it in the work, in his fearless approach to laying down paint. His painting gestures represented his enthusiasm: he always knew exactly where each of those broad brushstrokes was going. He controlled paint beautifully in those wide, seemingly loose, swaths of color. It very much expresses who he is." [5]

Kaplinski working from French easel for acrylics, Castlewood Canyon, Colorado 1976.

After Sandra Wilson sold her gallery in 1980, Jim Fisher, her one-time assistant, represented Kaplinski and his cohorts until his gallery closed. Then Tom Carson took up the baton for a few shows. By the 1980s, however, Carlson and Sharer had moved away, and the rest of the group, including Kaplinski, had become successful and settled. They each found new venues for exhibiting and marketing their work, but would never forget the ties that bound them. And they would always hold Sandra Wilson, who had represented them in their "golden years as a group," in high esteem. [6]

Around the time he showed with Sandra Wilson, Kaplinski's painting journeys took him on a return visit to South America, to Alaska, Canada and throughout the American West. Notwithstanding his lust for travel, Kaplinski never abandoned his affection for Colorado's vast rolling prairies and glorious snow-capped Rocky Mountain peaks. He would return to them each fall to lay claim to the gold of the mountain aspens and that of their prairie cousins—the cottonwoods. Fall colors and the season's long shadows find their way year after year into his paintings, yet scenes are not repeated, nor does he simply resort to comfortable color schemes and compositions of the past.

Plein-air treatment has dominated his fall excursions, often limited to a day or two, with studied avoidance of crowds of autumn colorists with easels paired or grouped as, seemingly, a barricade against the awesome sounds and color of nature which might otherwise envelop them.

One place in Colorado with a plentitude of subject matter for Kaplinski's plein-air work is Rocky Mountain National Park. To arrive at its gateway, Estes Park, from Elizabeth takes under three hours. Established in 1915 as the nation's tenth national park at the urging of naturalist, Enos Mills, the park bears testimony to the grandeur of the Rockies. A concentrate of montane wonderland, the 416 square miles of the park also contain riparian, subalpine and alpine ecosystems. With an area three times the size of metropolitan Denver, Rocky Mountain straddles the Continental Divide and ranks as the highest national park in the country—over one fourth of the land is above

Springtime Echo, acrylic on canvas, 16" x 20" 1985.

timberline. The park contains one of Colorado's well-known 14ers, Long's Peak (14,259 feet) and over 60 peaks measuring above 12,000 feet; the headwaters of the Colorado River and over 150 lakes and 450 miles of stream; and meadows, grassy valleys and forests of spruce, fir, pine and aspen—all supporting a myriad of plant and animal life.

Kaplinski's landscape interpretations and technique piqued Jerry Ravenscroft's interest. In the mid-1970s Ravenscroft, a dealer in Estes Park, handled Kaplinski's paintings, competing with Sandra Wilson in Denver for his best works. Ravenscroft became quite involved in the creative process, often visiting the same sites that Kaplinski painted, "to see how he had interpreted them." He found that "Kaplinski's works were expressive translations of nature—not mere reproductions—often emphasizing what I didn't initially see." [7]

Roadside Color Show and Pageant,
plein-air watercolor, 15" x 30" 2002.
Collection of Jenne Baldwin.

On site with Kaplinski constituted another experience in contrasts. Ravenscroft recalls one outing near Estes Park when he was invited to join Buffalo and Vicky. Kaplinski parked his truck, grabbed his paint box and paper and headed to a trail along an aspen-studded ridge. Vicky spread out more comfortably in the front seat and began to hum to herself, now and then quietly singing a verse or two. She made no move to traipse after her husband. Ravenscroft ran off to catch up with Kaplinski, found him seated cross-legged, pad in his lap, looking at a complex outcropping of rocks shrouded with brilliant aspen. There was an easy vista to his left which would have been the joy of any artist satisfied with creating predictable and pleasing scenes in the Colorado mountains involving huge expanses, carpeted with green, riddled with gold of the fall tundra.

The challenge was to the right. Kaplinski went at it ravenously, with quick and sure brush strokes, never stopping, always on the move from light to dark. Done, he cast the painting aside, exhausted, lay flat on his back, and without a word, closed his eyes—and slept.

CHAPTER 7 GLACIERS AND SUN GLINTS IN ALASKA

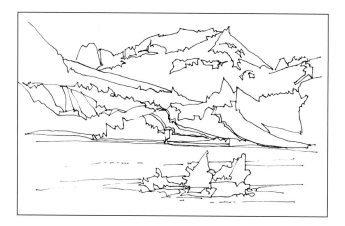

Glacier Bay, Alaska. **Drawing by Buffalo Kaplinski.**

With Vicky as his partner and fellow adventurer, Kaplinski found renewed vigor in his painting and new faith in himself. In the first years of their marriage she accompanied him on painting trips once or twice a year. Vicky's first lengthy excursion with her new husband was not to a place selected or outfitted by her, and tested the domestic bond between them. Traveling with Kaplinski is not for the fainthearted. The ice fields of Glacier Bay in Alaska provided his new wife with a glimpse of what plein-air meant to a frothing fanatic wielding a paintbrush.

In August 1978 the Kaplinskis flew to Juneau, Alaska, native land of the Tlinglit, once settled by Russians, then by gold miners in 1880. The working seaport with its harbor and many boat piers, the Russian Orthodox church, Tlingit totem poles, and two stunning peaks, Mt. Juneau and Mt. Roberts, rising in the background—none of these potential subjects lit fires under Kaplinski's brush. Only the mighty Mendenhall Glacier—13 miles distant, reaching 100 feet in height, measuring 1.5 miles wide and 6 miles long—garnered his attention. Like the prelude to a symphony, there lay his quarry: the magnificent glaciers of southeast Alaska.

After arriving in Juneau the plan was to make the 100-mile boat trip to Glacier Bay where Kaplinski would, from the deck of a commodious vessel or at stops along the way, record the grandeur of its ice fields and glaciers. Convenience, comfort, and the ordinary gave way to life-threatening encampment on an ice field with all the discomfort Mother Nature could provide. Kaplinski's idea of protection from inclement weather was a sheet of Visqueen big enough for two, art supplies, a couple of blankets, and a picnic basket containing lunch and dinner.

As the boat rounded into Glacier Bay, the first major tidewater glacier, Reid Glacier, came into view. The crisp lines of the glacier with glints of sun emphasizing its enormity gave way to a steady drizzle as the launch from the excursion boat dropped Vicky and Kaplinski off at its edge, then returned to

Mendenhall Glacier, **plein-air watercolor, 16" x 22" 2004.**

the ship where other passengers were already mourning the temporary loss of their traveling companions.

Kaplinski quickly hunkered down beneath the plastic cover and began to sketch. Vicky wept watching the profile of the excursion boat shrink as the distance between them spread. Moments later through her tears a vision appeared—a boat. Yes, *our* boat! They're coming back! Sure enough the launch headed for the glacier.

"You forgot your lunch basket!" yelled the helmsman through the mist.

The launch had barely come to rest when Vicky unloaded the meager supplies, patted Kaplinski on the shoulder, mumbled a brief compliment about the drawing, and scrambled aboard. Kaplinski was retrieved a day later—wet, cold, but inspired.

Curiosity had motivated the trip to Glacier Bay. Would it prove to be as spectacular as Kaplinski had been told? Everything about the 3,283,246-

Kaplinski's Alaska studio.

acre Glacier Bay National Park, designated as World Heritage Site in 1992, shouted grandeur. The place fairly vibrated with the awesome power of Nature. Kaplinski felt overwhelmed as he tried to grasp the imposing scale. In the distance, set against the mass of glaciers and peaking at 15,300 feet, Mount Fairweather teased his mind. The magnitude of Johns Hopkins Glacier, stretching 250 feet or 25 stories high, dwarfed Reid Glacier, a mere 150 feet, in more ways than one. Johns Hopkins also made a show of dropping icebergs into the bay, a process known as "calving off," which caused boats a mile distant to buck as the waves hit. The Tlinglit had a more colorful name. They called the groaning and creaking, then the crashing and booming of a tidewater glacier releasing huge chunks of ice "white thunder." The whole experience blew Kaplinski away: "Whoever envisioned massive chunks of ice floating around in the most bizarre, abstract shapes with manganese blue color saturation on a grand, spectacular scale. . . . Occasionally a bald eagle may perch on an ice flow and only then could I get a fix on the size."

Not only the immensity of scale confronted Kaplinski. How would he capture the complexity that naturalist John Muir had seen nearly one hundred years earlier when he explored the area with Tlinglit guides in boats? In *Travels in Alaska* (1879), Muir published his observations of glaciers with their "bewildering variety of novel architectural forms . . . glittering lance-tipped gables, and obelisks." He wrote about gorges, crevasses, grooves and hollows filled with light, "shimmering and throbbing in pale-blue tones of ineffable tenderness and beauty." With his usual intensity, watercolor began to splatter as Kaplinski sought to match in paint what Muir had captured with words. Hardly missing a moment of light, he created sketches for studio pieces and a few plein-air watercolors that only hint at the hardships under which some were created. Design realism at which Kaplinski is so adept allows the beauty of the place to mask its harshness. While vowing "never again!" Vicky recognized the subtleties in each plein-air work created by her husband suggest that a bout of foul weather or some other calamity was never far away.

The glaciers worked their enchantment on Kaplinski. He returned to southeast Alaska two years later—without Vicky—for whitewater rafting on the mighty Tatshenshini River. On this trip he wouldn't have the opportunity to paint. "We came upon the Malaspina . . . so large I could hardly seem to adjust my eyes to the overwhelming scale. Only when a raft was in front of the glacier, did I realize the overwhelming size." That's one that got away, but the Malaspina, Alaska's largest piedmont lobe glacier, an 850-square-mile monster more that half the size of Rhode Island, made its impression on Kaplinski. The manganese blue of Alaska's glaciers still haunts him, and he vowed to return once more to their homeland. [1]

The Surrounds of Glacier Bay, Alaska, acrylic on canvas, 40" x 30". Collection of Mr. and Mrs. Marshall Schield.

A Little More Ice, Please, Johns
Hopkins Glacier, Glacier Bay,
Alaska, watercolor, 21½" x
16½" 2004.

The Sounds and Scenes of National Parks: Canyons, Waterfalls, Plopping Mud Pots, and Geysers

While Kaplinski had found the subject matter in the state of Colorado that provided, and would continue to provide, rich opportunities for his paintings, the landscapes of Indian Country in New Mexico and Arizona drew him repeatedly to that area. Similarly, the natural wonders of the Utah canyon lands, the Grand Canyon, Yellowstone and Yosemite, which much like Cézanne's sixty versions of Mt. Sainte-Victoire, provided landscape features he would paint time and time again in a variety of renditions. Geological formations fascinated him. "It was the pure design of these things—the crisp edges and softer shadows they created that attracted me," Kaplinski recalled.

Man: A Trifle Among Mountains.
Drawing by Buffalo Kaplinski.

In August 1972 Kaplinski planned a painting trip from Evergreen, Colorado to northeastern Arizona and the flat-topped yellow sandstone tablelands of Hopi and stunning red sandstone of Navajo land. Years before he agreed to accompany Kaplinski on this trip, the paintings of Canyon de Chelly by Gerard Curtis Delano had lured George Carlson to northeastern Arizona. With this trip, the two artists expanded on the more localized forays they had made a few years earlier in the Taos area, and as usual debated on which vehicle to take. Deciding on Carlson's canary yellow Jeep Wagoneer, they packed their painting gear and initial doubts about the rain-making credentials of the Hopi, and headed for the snake dance at Oraibi on Arizona's Third Mesa. At the conclusion of the dance, the Snake Priests released assorted rattlesnakes and bull snakes, which slithered off to surrounding rocks and sparse underbrush, becoming like rivulets of the prayed-for rain. As the two artists pulled out of the parking area at the base of Third Mesa, one drop, then another, splattered against their dusty windshield. Was it simply a fortuitous cloud, or a symbol of hope and expectation that the Indian faithful were willing to share with their visitors?

From Hopi the artist duo journeyed to the canyons of the *Dineah*—the land of the Navajo. At Canyon de Chelly the sheer red cliffs forming the canyon's walls, the result of streams eroding compacted iron-rich sand dunes

Canyon de Chelly, watercolor, 24" x 18" 1995. Collection of Mr. and Mrs. Harmon S. Graves.

deposited over 200 million years ago, reached 1000 feet high. Their smooth walls yielded clefts here and there, which challenged the artist to work quickly as the sun marched steadily westward above the meandering river below while weaving new texture into the rich red sandstone walls. "The water stains streaking down the canyon walls," Kaplinski observed, "created patterns that truly enhanced the enormity of these quiet places."

In order to access Canyon de Chelly, Kaplinski and Carlson had to hire an authorized Navajo guide, Johnson John. He took them along various routes of the three-pronged canyon, and conducted them to various ruins, among them White House and Standing Cow, once inhabited by the ancient ones. Through Johnson John, however, they experienced more than just a painting adventure; they got an insight into Navajo life. When he discovered that Carlson was a sculptor, Johnson John encouraged the two artists to meet his father, Navajo John, a medicine man. Carlson spent the afternoon working on a portrait of the older man. When dusk came, Carlson and Kaplinski needed a place to sleep. Navajo John said it made no sense for them to drive all the way to Chinle, and invited them to spend the night in his hogan. Navajo John told them to pull up a sheepskin, indicating a four-foot-high stack, and find a spot on the clay floor. As night fell, other Navajo men began arriving. Each pulled a sheepskin from the pile and claimed a sleeping place on the clay. By the time the last Navajo arrived, the two artists figured they shared the floor with about a dozen men. Then the crowning moment. The last arrival, a city-dwelling Navajo, entered the hogan and said, "Whew, it smells like animals in here!" A hissing sound ensued as he pulled out a lilac-scented room deodorizer and began spraying. Kaplinski buried his laughter under his sheepskin. Carlson couldn't hold it and the whole hogan erupted with guffaws and complaints. Their amusement turned to wonder the next morning. Kaplinski and Carlson awoke to the only daylight in the hogan—sunbeams filtering in through the smoke hole at the top. The experience was primordial. It reminded Carlson of the interior of Mandan Indians' round, thatched-roof dwellings along the Missouri River, painted in the 1830s by explorer artists, Karl Bodmer and George Catlin.[1]

Leaving the towering walls of Canyon de Chelly, Kaplinski and Carlson pointed the Jeepster across Navajo land to northwest Arizona. Here they confronted perhaps the grandest of all scenes, the awesome Grand Canyon, one of the world's finest examples of arid-land erosion. Over millennia the weather and the stone-carving Colorado River gouged out this monumental canyon on the Colorado Plateau—227 miles long, 15 miles at its widest point, averaging 4000 feet in depth—and left a great chasm of unsurpassing beauty. Major John Wesley Powell, who led the second geological and geographical government survey of the Grand Canyon in 1872, accompanied by artist Thomas Moran, felt that even the combination of words and graphic art failed to portray one of nature's most sublime spectacles. His words, sometimes poetic, convey the excitement of initial scientific documentation of this geologic wonder:

> Climb the cliff at the end of Labyrinth Cañon and look over the plain below and you see vast numbers of buttes scattered about over scores of miles, and every butte so regular and beautiful that you can hardly cast aside the belief that they are works of Titanic art. . . . But no human hand has placed a block in all those wonderful structures. The rain drops of unreckoned ages have cut them all from the solid rock.[2]

In 1873 Thomas Moran, Kaplinski's childhood inspiration, wrote a descriptive letter of his first view of the Grand Canyon from the Tororeap vantage point:

Foundations of The Earth – Job 38:4, plein-air acrylic on canvas, 30" x 40", Grand Canyon, Arizona 1979. Private collection.

The whole gorge for miles lay beneath us and it was by far the most awfully grand and impressive scene that I have ever yet seen. . . . Above and around us rose a wall of 2000 feet and below us a vast chasm 2500 feet in perpendicular depth and ½ mile wide. At the bottom the river, very muddy and seemingly only a hundred feet wide, seemed slowly moving along but in reality is a rushing torrent filled with rapids. A suppressed sort of roar comes up constantly from the chasm but with that exception everything impresses you with an awful stillness. The color of the Great Cañon itself is red, a light Indian Red, and the material sandstone and red marble and is in terraces all the way down. All about the canon is variously colored sandstone mainly a light flesh or cream color and worn into very fine forms. [3]

As he viewed the Grand Canyon for the first time, Kaplinski must have felt the same overwhelming awe. All the colors and values, and tremendous shapes and forms of Grand Canyon's buttes and valleys now begged Kaplinski's interpretation. The task facing him was daunting. Yet Moran and some of the best American canyon painters who preceded him had managed to reduce its majesty to canvas and paper. Self-doubt intervened as Kaplinski's pencil sketched in a sun-lit ridge and the distant floor of the canyon below. Then, like a skier at the edge of a cornice, picturing in his mind only the first turn to be negotiated into the untracked powder snow below, and relying on his ability to develop a rhythm to reach the valley floor without consciously charting his route, Kaplinski began with the soft pale pink of the distant north rim working fast to the rich red crisp-lined, rock in mid-field, trusting that the scene would develop without dictating its course.

The artist at the canyon rim, Grand Canyon, Arizona 1979.

Kaplinski and Carlson finished their trip on a Grand Canyon high, both of them exhilarated by the canyon lands' geological formations—crisp at dawn, soft and shadowy at evening. With his tendency to revisit a favorite painting location, Kaplinski returned later on a solo trip to paint the South Rim. On that trip he painted *Foundations of the Earth – Job 38:4*, from Moran Point, a vista named after the illustrious artist. It seemed fitting homage to his earliest hero. Kaplinski's fascination with canyon lands also took him north of the Grand Canyon to Utah.

Initially in the early 1970s, he went in search of "Utah funk" in the state's old ranches and antique buildings. A thoughtful study of Kaplinski's *Utah Homestead – John Cracker* offers an insight into Cracker's soul and character, poignantly laid bare in Clarice (Kaplinski) Estes' verse:

John Cracker let the screen door bang,
Shivering on its hinges. He walked
unsure and sightless into a
buckskin morning; filled his pipe
from memory; squatted cracking
kneed; pushing black oak
from his old and fawning mind.

Another time, long ago, the pastures
fanned in quarter time. Mary, Mary,
silver ear bobs dancing.
John Cracker sat in reverie; his limp
hide vest flapping in the wind like
withered eagle wings.

Utah Homestead – John Cracker, **acrylic/
watercolor, 18" x 30" 1973. Private
collection.**

Later, over the next decade, he made several other painting trips to
Utah, drawn by the incredible forms of Arches, Bryce, Zion and Goblin Valley. In his younger, wilder years he saw erotic shapes of women in the bizarre
forms of Goblin Valley. At Bryce with its remarkable amphitheater, Kaplinski
was drawn to the towering spires called "hoodoos," formed from the erosion
of colorful limestones, sandstones and mudstones. The contrasting forms, colors and textures of Arches with its towering spires, balanced rocks, fins and
pinnacles and over 2000 natural sandstone archways found expression in his
brushes. In Zion, an ancient Hebrew word meaning a place of sanctuary, the
sunset-lit crimsons, tans and oranges of carved canyons, towering cliffs and
massive stone monoliths inspired several paintings.

For all the enchantment of the Southwest's canyon lands, Kaplinski
gave equal time to other areas to the west and north. Drawn always to the
one-of-a-kind landscape, Kaplinski naturally gravitated to national parks of
the Rocky Mountain West. Touted by James Bryce, former British ambassador
to the United States, as "the best idea America ever had," these national parks
with their canyons, peaks, waterfalls, tundra, and atmosphere beckoned to

Colorado River Canyonlands, **acrylic on paper, 19½" x 31". Collection of Mark Perry.**

Kaplinski and whoever of his artistic pals would willingly endure deprivation of the kind commonly associated with his travels.

Another seasoned painting pal, Len Chmiel, had painted with Kaplinski in Colorado and New Mexico. Bonded by a common Polish heritage, the two landscape painters also shared a passion for working on the spot. Chmiel remembered one short trip the two made from Denver to Arroyo Seco, a few miles from Taos, New Mexico, in 1974. They had made this excursion in winter, and the weather was so cold that they couldn't work outside or the paint would freeze. Kaplinski had four or five acrylics going simultaneously within the confines of Chmiel's van. "He had a mean snap to clear his brush of paint, and left paint spots all over my van." [4] Not bothered by the decorating job Kaplinski had done, Chmiel soon packed up his van for another painting duet.

Kaplinski and Chmiel—"L. Chmiel" as Kaplinski labeled him, converting his painting signature into a convenient moniker—loaded Chmiel's white Ford van and headed for Yellowstone National Park in 1975. Entering Yellowstone, Kaplinski and Chmiel found in the gigantic volcanic basin the same thousands of hot springs, steaming vents, fumaroles, paint pots, plopping mud

The Master's Touch, **plein-air watercolor, 16" x 20" 1985.**

pots and gushing geysers that the mountain men had reported in the early 1800s. John Colter, the first mountain man to see and describe the geothermal phenomena, was dismissed as a madman, and his discovery was mocked and called "Colter's Hell." Several decades later, when Ferdinand Hayden led a government survey expedition to the area in 1871, he verified Colter's claims. The steaming geysers and bubbling mud caldrons not only existed, Hayden had proof of them through the photographs of William Henry Jackson and the watercolors of Thomas Moran. While Jackson's black-and-white photos provided "scientific" proof, Moran's brilliant watercolors captured the beauty and color of Yellowstone. Based on the pictures and Hayden's geological report Congress decided to preserve the area for the American public in 1872.

The yellow-stoned canyon walls, a rainbow of rhyolite, provoked Rudyard Kipling to exclaim, "The sides of that gulf [are] one wild welter

Kaplinski and Len Chmiel packed and ready.

of color—crimson, emerald, cobalt, ochre, amber, honey splashed with port-wine, snow white, vermilion, lemon, and silver-grey, in wide washes." Thomas Moran complained, "These beautiful tints were beyond the reach of human art." [5] Despite those words, he rose to the challenge with aplomb, portraying Yellowstone's canyons and waterfalls, and mud pots and geysers. Considered some of Moran's best works, his virtuoso watercolors, done on the spot at Yellowstone, successfully captured the "wild welter" of colors that Kipling described. [6]

Yet even Thomas Moran had his doubts, as he worked on his first "Big Picture" of the Grand Cañon of the Yellowstone. This massive painting, measuring 7 feet by 12 feet, exacted all his artistic abilities: "I have always held that the Grandest, Most Beautiful, or Wonderful in Nature, would, in capable hands, make the grandest, most beautiful, or wonderful pictures, and that the business of a great painter should be the representation of great scenes in Nature. All the characteristics attach to the Yellowstone region, and if I fail to prove this, I fail to prove myself worthy [of] the name of paint. I cast all my claims to being an Artist, into this one picture of the Great Cañon and am

Sulphur Air and Pine Specters, **acrylic on board, 28 ½" x 23" 1976. Collection of Dr. and Mrs. Arthur Strasburger.**

willing to abide by the judgement upon it." [7] In gambling all he had in him, Moran must have been relieved to receive recognition that he had met his visual challenge. In the spring of 1872, the United States government purchased his painting, its first American landscape by an American artist, and unveiled it to public acclaim shortly after publicizing the designation of Yellowstone as the country's first national park.

As a colorist, Kaplinski had before him the same sights as Thomas Moran, his early hero, who must have also taken some deep breaths before aiming his brushes at the awe-inspiring wonders of Yellowstone. Expressing what he experienced in Yellowstone, and what confronted him some years later in Cedar Breaks National Monument in Utah, Kaplinski confessed that, "in reality the effect of light and color was actually more intense than [I] could possibly capture in pigment." [8]

Kaplinski soon set his sights on Yellowstone's natural features. Contemplating one of the park's most well-known landmarks, Old Faithful, he felt the immediacy of the gushing geyser could only be captured in watercolor or acrylic. After painting Old Faithful, Kaplinski moved to the north geyser basin, more colorful for its sulphur and mineral deposits, where he worked with an intensity to match the landscape. As seriously as he took his painting, his famous sense of humor worked its way into his paintings. Entranced with the action and sounds of a geyser, he titled a four-paneled painting on the subject "Bloop." [9]

The bubbling mud pots and steaming vents of the geyser basin, vied with the Grand Canyon of the Yellowstone and waterfalls on the Yellowstone River, offering Kaplinski and Chmiel abundant subjects to choose from. Here Mother Nature's palette challenged these two apostles of brilliant color. As Kaplinski and Chmiel wandered through Yellowstone, not only was the depiction of color constantly testing their abilities, but the scene selections provoked a recurring dialogue between the two artists.

"Look at this," one would exclaim, "do you want to paint here?"

"Naw, let's drive on and see what's ahead."

"How can you pass it by? It's tugging at me."

And so it would go until the driver in a sudden exercise of dominion and control would say, "This is it. Paint or sit!"

Besides their passion for the landscape, the Polish comrades had another commonality. As a release from the intensity of painting, a warped sense of humor engaged them, and others within ear-shot or sight. Chmiel recalled standing in line at the Yellowstone Falls grocery store when suddenly Kaplinski blurted out: "So, why did your parole officer let you off?" Taken aback for a split second, Chmiel played along, leaving a nervous clerk and a worried next-in-line customer.

Out on the winding park roads it took only the mischievous point of a finger by either of them to cause tourists driving behind them to look where they were pointing, come to an abrupt stop, and search for an anticipated bear, waterfall, or soaring eagle, then be jarred into reality by a bump from a following motorist drawn into the search.

Most of their time, however, was spent immersed in producing on-the-spotters. At the end of the day, while storing paints, brushes, paper, board and canvas, the inevitable question was, "Well, what did you find out there?" Seated on back bumper of the van, Kaplinski would offer a study of some of the park's magnificence. Chmiel would nod and reflect—Wow! I never saw

El Capitan, watercolor, 40" x 30" 1978.
Collection of Denver Public Library,
Western History Department.

that. The role, of course, was reversed the next day.

Despite moments of doubt and subtle competition, Chmiel and Kaplinski provided a lively, colorful, technically solid record of Yellowstone worthy of the acclaim accorded them in their exhibition at Sandra Wilson Galleries in Denver in February 1976.

Three years later Kaplinski ventured further west to Yosemite National Park. While smaller than Yellowstone, it is home to so many of the geological mistresses Kaplinski embraced. An area of superlative beauty, the sky-scraping cliffs and pinnacles of Yosemite Valley provide the backdrop for spectacular waterfalls, including the magnificent Yosemite Falls, plunging down 2,425 feet, the highest waterfall in North America.

A favorite Yosemite ranger yarn contrasts the priorities of the artist and the tourist. "I'm here for an hour—what should I see?" inquired a new visitor of a seasoned park ranger. The artist, of course, sees millenniums, a cacophony of color and movement. The ranger, providing an answer to the tourist's question after reflecting for a moment, can only respond, "I suppose if I only had an hour to spend at Yosemite, I'd just walk over there by the river and sit down and cry!" [10]

With so many tantalizing subjects inviting his interpretive skills—lofty granite mountains, glacier-scoured valleys, backcountry dotted with lakes and flowers, and racing wilderness rivers—Kaplinski felt compelled to pay homage

Storm Over Yoho, British Columbia,
plein-air watercolor, 12" x 30" 2000.
Collection of Steve "Grizzly" Adams.

to three well-known sites that had drawn California's Yosemite artist, Thomas Hill, to paint repeatedly over several decades. Kaplinski's version of Half Dome, a massive monolith standing 4800 feet high, might frustrate a technical climber in search of traditional ascents, yet stir the emotions of anyone who has visited this site. And who could resist its sister peak, El Capitan, a sheer granite wall rising up nearly 4000 feet from the valley floor below. Last but just as lovely, even from the distant tourist stop, the dramatic Bridal Veil Falls.

Kaplinski's *Half Dome at High Noon* was featured at Sandra Wilson Galleries in 1979 among his works documenting travels through the canyon lands of Utah and Arizona and far reaches of Yosemite National Park. The following year Reno's Stremmel Galleries held a solo exhibition of Kaplinski's works, *Yosemite and Beyond.* The Stremmel Gallery brochure featured forty-five of his paintings. It provided a review of the artist's works, dubbing them "a series of Western landscapes as bold and dramatic as the country itself. In a sense it is a journey, starting with and concentrating on the grandeur of Yosemite National Park, as seen from the valley floor, to the last rays of sunlight on the tip of El Capitan. . . . Kaplinski's exhilaration expands beyond Yosemite and the Sierras, to the powerful images of the great Southwest, and finally up into the Rockies." [11]

By the late 1970s art critics noted a change in Kaplinski's work. A review of his solo show at Sandra Wilson Galleries in April 1978 in the *Rocky Mountain News* noted a new "boldness missing in earlier work" and attention to the "subtle textural differences in nature—the translucence of a spring sky—the patterns of a stormy sky." The more monochromatic approach had been replaced with a full color palette. Kaplinski remarked on these stylistic changes: "I see color in a different way today. I have simplified my approaches. It used to be I would block out colors." [12] A year later a Denver Post critic remarked on Kaplinski's highly colorful paintings—exhilarating documents of the artist's recent travels—through terrain he had visited and painted before: Yosemite and the canyon lands of Utah and Arizona. This new body of work at the Sandra Wilson Gallery showed how an artist could bring a new vision to familiar subject matter. The reviewer remarked on the artist's bold use of color in a new painting, *Sunfire Glow*, of Utah's Cedar Breaks National Monument.

In the fall of 1981, the Carson Gallery of Western American Art featured Kaplinski's recent landscapes of the American West. A new subject—the Tetons with its distinctive jagged mountains and spectacular peaks—made its first debut among the familiar old standbys: Canyon de Chelly, Shiprock, the Colorado Rockies, and Alaska. As before, Kaplinski had taken time to interpret America's national treasures, yet the Carson exhibition ushered in a new era for Kaplinski. He had spent fifteen years honing his brushes on the West's wondrous geological forms. In his tireless pursuit of new and exciting subject matter, his wanderlust had broadened. He longed for new horizons beyond the Americas.

Kaplinski sensed that his interpretations of any scene should not draw upon wholly familiar techniques and composition, nor should his subject matter be limited to the familiar scenes of the Southwest. The recognized conundrum of any artist was, of course, whether the artist should paint to meet the perceived desires of his established patrons, or allow the artist's interpretation of whatever landscape inspires him to dictate his destiny. Kaplinski chose the latter. He would soon become immersed in the history of Greece, the grandeur of its antiquities, and the brilliance of its atmosphere. A stirring change in palette and subject matter was about to occur.

GREECE AND TURKEY: RHODES' COLOSSUS TO CAPPADOCIA'S CHURCHES

Architecture and its relation to the spectacular landscapes of the Greek Islands and Turkey became the focus of Kaplinski's 1983 travels. In March and April he and Vicky, whose recollections of their Alaska journey had by then dimmed sufficiently, planned to visit islands in the Aegean Sea, then cross over to Turkey from Rhodes. When they landed in Athens, the Kaplinskis immediately experienced an "overwhelming sense of history." Perhaps in no other place in the world is the synergy between man's structures and their settings so evident. Here, in the time of the ancient Greeks, temples were designed and placed in harmony with the landscape—one suitable for the god of sea and horses, another for the god of war, still another for the goddess of love. [1]

Steps and Domes In Greece.
Drawing by Buffalo Kaplinski.

The artist interpreting these places is not free to ignore twenty-five hundred years of history, but whatever interpretive limitations arise are, in part, offset by the power of the scene which alone lends importance to the painting.

Kaplinski on location in Patmos, Greece.

Windmill Soliloquy, Turn, Turn, Turn,
acrylic on board, 21" x 17" 1984.

Athens and its Acropolis could not deter the Kaplinskis from their true destination. Island-hopping excursion boats soon ferried them over the azure Aegean Sea to Paros, Mykonos, Santorini, Patmos, Samos, and Rhodes. Although well inured to capturing the harsh, bright light of the Southwest, the dazzling light of the Greek islands sparkling on pristine white-washed buildings presented unfamiliar subject matter in a new light. Added to the challenge, each island had its own history, its own particular atmosphere. Determined to portray the unique qualities of each, Kaplinski set his focus on architectural motifs. He removed himself from the highly trafficked areas and wandered the side streets and back alleys in search of new themes. Byzantine domes, bell towers, ancient stairways zigzagging their way from one level to the other of towns hugging the rugged coastline as well as churches, cottages, and some of the colorful inhabitants of these sun-drenched environments all found their way into Kaplinski's plein-air acrylic and watercolor compositions. His approach was direct, relying on the boldness of the blues of the sky and sea, softened by carefully chosen warmer hues for shadows and surrounding landscapes.

The Meek Shall Inherit The Earth, **acrylic on canvas, 18" x 24" 1983. Private collection.**

Two islands in particular, Santorini and Paros, piqued Kaplinski's artistic and historical interest. The most dramatic feature of Santorini, officially known as Thyra, is the island's caldera. Sometime around 1450 BC its volcanic heart exploded, leaving a bow-shaped rim of cliffs and two remnant isles that form an open lagoon 37 miles long. Equally explosive, Thyra's history is reflected today in sites such as Akrotiri, the "prehistoric Pompeii" of the Aegean, the ancient city of Thira and a Roman church dating to the tenth century. In Paros' capital, modern Italianate houses and gardens of oranges and pomegranates contrasted with the remains of a medieval castle and the ruins of ancient marble temples and sites. During the classical age, the startling white stone from Paros was sought after by Greek architects and sculptors. The island's chief source of wealth in ancient times, Paros marble was used for buildings and statues in distant Athens and other cities. Two famous examples, the Venus de Milo and the Parian Marble (or Parian Chronical),

Stairway In Greece, acrylic on canvas, 18" x 24" 1983. Private collection.

a marble tablet outlining early and classical Greek history, grew out of stone from mines still quarried in Paros today. In these echoes of Thyra's ancient and turbulent past, and the luminous white stone works of Paros, Kaplinski found new inspiration for his brushes.

In Rhodes Kaplinski entered a realm of mythic proportion in Rodos (Rhodes City), the island's capital. In the Old City, vestiges of Europe's Middle Ages—a moat, walls and buildings like the Palace of the Knights from the tenth- and eleventh-century Crusader era—contrasted sharply with the Suleymaniye mosque (predominately nineteenth century) and the Rijep Pasha (1558) from the times of the Ottoman Empire. Although archeological findings date the history of Rhodes back to the Middle Bronze Age, one of the island's most notable landmarks arose from the time of Classical Greece: the Colossus of Rhodes, one of the Seven Wonders of the Ancient World. Completed around 280 BC, the giant bronze statue stood 110 feet high. Built in honor of Helios, the Grecian sun god, the Colossus beamed out over the sea for 65 years until a giant earthquake toppled it. Commenting two centuries later on the size of the remaining ruins, the Roman scholar, Pliny, wrote that few people could make their arms meet around the statue's thumb. When Arabian forces raided Rhodes around 650 AD, they ordered the statue broken up, and sold the bronze as scrap metal—a supposed 900 camel-loads worth. With its remnants long since vanished, Kaplinski chose to portray the two famous bronze deer on high pedestal columns flanking Madraki Harbor, which now mark the spot the Colossus reputedly once occupied.

Another of Rodos' highlights, the eighteenth-century Turkish baths, bore testimony to the days of the Ottoman Empire and spoke of the island's proximity to Asia. From Rhodes the Kaplinskis could see the brown coastline of Turkey, their next destination. After a boat ride to Kusadasi, they visited Turkey's greatest archeological site: the ruins of Ephesus. This important Ionian city, founded in the third century BC, later became the Roman capital of Asia Minor. Today Ephesus is one of the best-preserved classical cities on the Medi-

Where Colossus Stood, watercolor, 12" x 8½" 1986. Collection of Mr. and Mrs. Tom Lord.

Istanbul, Turkey. **Drawing by Buffalo Kaplinski.**

terranean Sea. The Kaplinskis walked along the mile-long marble road built in the fifth century AD, leading from the port to magnificent ruins including Hadrian's Temple and the gigantic Great Theater (seating capacity 24,000). Kaplinski eagerly set up to paint important sites, including the ruins of temple of the Greek goddess Artemis (Diana), the second of the Seven Wonders of the Ancient World he encountered on this trip.

Returning to Denver via Athens, Kaplinski completed a few studio pieces, then exhibited his Greek treasures the following October at The Deer Dancer in Denver. Critics commented favorably on the new work. The *Rocky Mountain News* noted: "The Greek Kaplinski is a more carefree painter. There are none of the intense color values that have at times seemed almost electrifying in his Southwest work. The rugged landscapes, with their dramatic thrusts and planes, have given way to a show devoted to the striking architecture of a country steeped in history. . . . The artist concentrates on the architecture and its relation to nature without trying to interpret moods." [2] In a dramatic departure from his usual style, the paintings from this trip no longer included the elements used in depicting the Southwest. Instead of familiar warm-hued colors, Kaplinski used a cool palette, "predominantly in freshly scrubbed white and gradations of blue, with occasional forays into the warmer tones of the spectrum." [3] The highest praise, however, came from collectors when the exhibition sold out. Success from his foray to the Aegean lived beyond the exhibition: Kaplinski got commissions to repaint the whole series.

This happy turn of events allowed Kaplinski to make a second trip to Turkey in 1999. The visit to Ephesus whetted Kaplinski's appetite to see more of the country that culturally and physically serves as a bridge between Europe and Asia. Although he read up on Turkey and had gotten his feet wet depicting magnificent ruins of the dry, dusty climate of Ephesus, nothing quite prepared Kaplinski for the wonders of Istanbul.

With its three-thousand-year history, the former Constantinople served as capital to both the Byzantine and the Ottoman Empires. A mixture of Islamic and Western traditions, today's Istanbul is recognized as Turkey's cultural and business center. The Grand Bazaar alone—with its oriental atmosphere, over four thousand shops, and streets named after its traders in silver, gold, carpets, slippers, boots and books—would have been daunting enough. Overwhelmed by the city's vast size and bustling millions, Kaplinski found refuge from the busy commercial districts in old Istanbul's Sultanahmet. Within the perimeters he found some of the city's most important architectural gems. He marveled at the magnitude of the Aya Sofya (the Church of Holy Wisdom), started under the Emperor Justinian in 532 AD, who intended to create Christendom's grandest church; and the sprawling Topkapi Palace, to the northeast, testimony to the opulence of the sultans. Captivated by the beauty of the Blue Mosque with its six minarets and cascade of domes and half-domes, Kaplinski happened to see it at night, lit by a shower of fireworks. He preserved the moment in *Fireworks over Istanbul Mosque,* and in *Nighttime Reflections – Istanbul Mosque.* As with Istanbul

Fireworks over Istanbul Mosque, **watercolor, 16" x 12" 1999. Collection of Mr. and Mrs. Mike Hurshman.**

Nighttime Reflections – Istanbul Mosque,
**watercolor, 16" x 12" 1999. Collection of
Jean Chrest.**

itself, the mosques worked a magical spell on Kaplinski. He considered these Islamic beauties among the most interesting subjects; and painted several others, including the Suleiman Mosque reflected in water.

Exhausted from painting Istanbul's magnificence, the over-stimulated Kaplinski worked his way into the heartland of Turkey where he encountered the almost-comical landscapes of Cappadocia. As one enters this remarkable province there is a sense that Mother Nature refused to be taken for granted, and created what causes the visitor to stand, hands-on-hip, and utter, "Astounding!" Thousands of years ago eruptions of porous rock covered the landscape. Erosion sculpted what now appear as cones, pinnacles, towering toadstools, and pyramids. The porous rock yielded readily to picks and shovels, and homes and churches were carved from Cappadocia's wondrous rock. These troglodyte houses provided defenses against marauders, and the walls of the rock churches offered a perfect setting for the colorful frescos telling the biblical story in continuous friezes.

Kaplinski's outdoor technique must have added one more curiosity for tourists wandering through this sculptured landscape where for centuries time

Open Air Museum of Goreme, **watercolor, 12" x 20½" 1999.**

has stood still. He works rapidly, his face close to the surface of his work, his eyes appearing to squint almost closed, rarely pausing. The Mad Hatter painting the tea party!

Never quite a tourist himself, perhaps more like Alice in Wonderland, Kaplinski played the role of passionate observer, distilling his experiences and the spirit of foreign lands visited into paint on paper. The artist's initial trip to Greece and Turkey would open the way for him to journey to other countries far removed from his beloved Southwest. His work had changed dramatically under the Mediterranean sun. Foreign travels always brought new impetus to his work. In 1984, less than a year after his visit to Greece and Turkey, Kaplinski's work would undergo another astonishing change—one tied to and almost as significant as the life-changing event that led to his next journey: a visit to the Holy Land.

CHAPTER 10

THE MIDDLE EAST: RIVER NILE TO THE DOME OF THE ROCK

In 1977 Kaplinski, desperate for help with renovations on the ranch, and no longer able to find fellow hippies to work for him, had hired eighteen-year-old Terry Wilson. Some time later Wilson revealed that he was a born-again Christian and began to talk of the Lord and Jesus. This aggravated Kaplinski, who thought of Wilson as "one of those holier-than-thou" people, yet he was hesitant to dismiss the young man since he had such a good work ethic. Then Wilson invited Kaplinski to the Baptist Church in Elizabeth. Kaplinski, who wore his hair long and espoused the revolutionary ideas of the 1960s, went just to show those "self-righteous Christians." His hostile attitude dissolved in the face of their acceptance of him. That the congregation would reach out to a long-haired hippie surprised him.

Raised a Roman Catholic by his parents, Kaplinski later questioned religion and other philosophies and rebelled against them. "As I saw religion, it seemed merely stupid bondage." His opinion eroded, however, as he continued to attend church services in Elizabeth and came to the realization that: "My life [had been] an offense to the living God. . . . I started to believe that Jesus Christ came as my savior." On February 2, 1978, Kaplinski was born again.

Six years later Kaplinski planned a trip to the Middle East. Although always in search of new subject matter, this next international trip would also fulfill a long-held dream to visit the Holy Land. He had rediscovered Christianity in himself, and would now travel to see and experience places important to the life of his beloved Christ. On March 5, 1984, he departed for Jordan, Egypt, and the area now known as Israel.

Kaplinski began his two-month odyssey in Jordan with the primary purpose of visiting the ancient metropolis of Petra, southwest of Amman. Dating back to Neolithic times, Petra served as capital city to the Nabataeans beginning around 300 BC. It fell to the Romans in 104 AD, and became their stronghold in Arabia. Strategically located on a major travel route that connected Africa and Arabia with Damascus, the city flourished as the center of the spice and incense trade. Abandoned by the cultures and traders that made it flourish, the familiar Treasury and the Temple El-Dier at the northern end of Petra reminds the visitor that a grand civilization once prospered here.

To get to Petra, Kaplinski wended his way through the mile-long Siq gorge, a deep ravine too narrow for beasts of burden. Eons ago the waters of the Wadi Musa (Spring of Moses) had carved out a split in the mountain, leaving canyon walls 30 stories high. Then through a chink in the Siq's dark walls, sunlight illuminated the rose-colored walls of the Treasury, a masterpiece of Nabataean architecture. Hand chiseled out of sandstone, this Hellenistic jewel with its two tiers of Corinthian columns, towered one-hundred-thirty feet high above Kaplinski. He had found his first subject. Reluctant to simply reproduce the magnificence of the Treasury in detail, which the history of the site commands, Kaplinski shrouded the site in a monochromatic mystery inviting the viewer to consider the glorious past and dismiss its present state.

Petra: Rose-Colored City, The Treasury, **watercolor, 34" x 26". Collection of Mr. and Mrs. Doug Phillips.**

Eager to explore the rest of the city, he hiked the main thoroughfare to view its other great first-century BC temples, palaces, tombs, towers, and colonnades. Exploring outside the city, he made the arduous climb to the Monastery, Petra's best-preserved monument. Petra's sandstone cliffs, the most unusual walls Kaplinski had ever seen, reminded the artist of Canyon de Chelly. Both had reddish rock in common, and similar variegated colors—blues, crimsons, reds and yellow-ochres—which often combined to produce marbleized effects. Like the Navajo living among the ruins at Canyon de Chelly, Bedouins still use the dwellings at Petra. [1]

Within the ruins, he found caves to explore; among local inhabitants Kaplinski met and established a good rapport with some local Jordanians and

Kaplinski with Mohammed Ahmeol Abed – his guide.

some "very interesting, very happy" Bedouin tribespeople. Towards the end of his five-day stay, he became acquainted with Selah, a small Kuwaiti man who looked like Anwar Sadat. Selah had come to Petra to make a video of the area. The two men hit it off, and Kaplinski got a taste of real Arabic hospitality. Selah bought Kaplinski some meals, then drove him, as a favor, to Amman to catch a plane to Cairo.

Next on the schedule: Cairo, the "Jewel of the Orient," a world of ancient mosques, medieval forts, and fifteen-hundred-year-old markets. The teeming life of the city, its architecture and "complete funkiness" overwhelmed Kaplinski. Walking its busy streets, he observed Arabs from all over the world with their flowing robes, colorful kofiahs, and turbans; donkeys next to trucks on the road, and people driving the wrong way down a one-way street; shops selling roasted seeds and nuts right next to a grimy mechanic shop. After taking in the sights, including the Mosque of Mohammed Ali, built in 1830, and towering over the city from the high perch of the famous Citadel, and the place where Joseph, Mary and the Baby Jesus lived, he ventured into Cairo's environs. A young guide took him to a pottery village with giant kilns; then his taxi driver, Saad, drove him to Giza. He spent two days there exploring and painting, and taking in the Sphinx and the pyramids—and the only Seventh Wonder of the Ancient World still standing: the Great Pyramid of Giza.

Donkeys loaded with Kaplinski's painting supplies and travel gear led by Mohammed Ahmeol Abed in the Valley of the Kings.

From Cairo Kaplinski flew to Luxor, his home base for visiting the Valley of the Kings, and the tombs of the Pharoahs. Not wanting to take a taxi or partake in the "tour of turkeys," he was standing outside the hotel, trying to figure out alternative transportation. A small, older, white-turbaned Arab wearing a *balbalaya,* or long robe, approached him, asking if he needed a guide. Kaplinski's prayers were answered in Mohammed Ahmeol Abed, who owned two donkeys. Loading backpack, paint boxes, water and camera, artist and guide eschewed blacktop roads for trails. They crossed over steep passes in full blasting sun and ninety-five degree heat, dismounting and walking when the footing became treacherous or too steep. "Just like in biblical times," Kaplinski arrived on the back of a donkey in the Valley of the Kings. He and Mohammed entered through the one narrow gorge that served as its security gate—which ultimately proved ineffective against the ancient robbers of these treasure-laden tombs. The valley, shaped like splayed fingers of the human hand, was the burial site of choice of the great pharaohs of Egypt between 1509 and 1078 BC.

Mohammed waited patiently while Kaplinski visited the tombs and paid homage to Tutankhamun, then sent the donkeys over rough trails to get an aerial view of Queen Hatshepsut's temple. The small party made the descent into the valley, and while Mohammed watched the donkeys and the gear, Kaplinski explored the temple of the fifth ruler of the Eighteenth Dynasty, who declared herself pharaoh in 1473 BC. After touring around the Valley of the Kings, Kaplinski hired Mohammed to accompany him to Karnak, the massive

Tea Time – Valley of The Kings, plein-watercolor, 20" x 16" 1984.

complex of temples, covering over 64,000 square feet, built as a place of worship in Theban times, and added to over a thirteen-hundred-year time span; and to the temple of Luxor, built to honor the family of Amon-Re, the Egyptian equivalent of Zeus, by King Amenhotep who reigned from 1390-1353 BC.

By now artist and guide had established a routine. Kaplinski would explore the area and take photographs while deciding on a painting location. He would then set up his easel and paint while Mohammed stood guard. On one occasion, typical of many, Kaplinski had completed his rendition of the scene before him and was standing, arms folded, giving the work a final check. Mohammed approached and without inflection remarked, "He is going now".

"Who's doing what?" Kaplinski inquired, thinking he had been so absorbed in his work and hadn't noticed a visitor.

"He is not painting and he goes now".

"Oh, I get it—it's time for us to pack up?"

"Yes, he goes now."

Always the same ritual—never ceasing to draw a smile as Kaplinski washed out his paint tray and packed up his supplies.

While doing some small figure studies and a night scene of the mosque and temple of Luxor, Kaplinski and his protector Mohammed drew a crowd of about twenty. Even under Mohammed's watchful eye, pencils and paint

Sheik Ali's Fly - Infested Oasis, **plein-air watercolor, 8½" x 11½" 1985. Collection of the artist.**

brushes would occasionally slip unnoticed from Kaplinski's art box into the hands of inquisitive children of the desert.

Savvy to what the artist wanted, Mohammed took Kaplinski to places tourists never set foot in. Through Mohammed, Kaplinski got to see "out" villages where people painted memories of trips to Mecca on the walls and get invited into homes for tea. At Sheik Ali's oasis, Mohammed found an area that encapsulated all of the elements Kaplinski wanted to paint, many reminiscent of the American Southwest. Here the artist found the soft earth tones of the arid hills contrasting with the white stucco of Sheik Ali's residence which blazed in the sunlight, but converted to a cool gray-violet in the shade. The patchwork of irrigated land surrounding the buildings appeared as an emerald isle—man's courageous challenge to the ever-encroaching desert. What an inviting scene! Yet within those charming walls so gracefully shaded by stately palms was the most filthy, fly-infested restaurant Kaplinski and Mohammed encountered in Egypt. All of this disturbing realism is nowhere to be found in Kaplinski's elegant plein-air watercolor of this scene so welcoming to the desert traveler.

From Luxor Kaplinski flew to Aswan, the site of the first cataract of the Nile, and jumping off point for Abu Simbel near the second cataract and Egypt's border with Sudan. A set of two temples—the Great Temple and the Small Temple—stand to honor the pharaoh Ramesses II, who reigned during the thirteenth century BC, and his favorite wife, Nefertari. Viewing the four rock-carved sandstone statues of the Great Temple, rising sixty-seven feet high, and the thirty-three-foot-high statues—two of Ramesses and one of Nefertari—flanking the temples' facades, Kaplinski had a hard time figuring out what to paint. Deciding to stay in Abu Simbel overnight, he got to see and paint the nighttime illumination and the sunlight dawning on these great monuments. Then back to Cairo to absorb more of that city and get one last glimpse of the pyramids before flying to Israel.

As Kaplinski left behind those historic Arab sites, What was his interpretation to be of those places which are historically tied to Muslim, Jew, and Christian? What of the Temple Mount in Jerusalem, where by Biblical accounts Abraham nearly sacrificed his son Isaac before God intervened; where Jesus cast out the moneychangers; and the Prophet Muhammad by scriptural accounts ascended to heaven? As Kaplinski entered a land of biblical proportion to visit places connected to Christ, these would all be interpreted in some fashion according to his faith.

After landing in Tel Aviv, Kaplinski stayed long enough to have his nervousness about terrorists and rumors of unfriendly Israelis dispelled by the charm of the people in this modern center of commerce and culture. He went to see Old Jaffa, site of one of the world's oldest ports; and the Museum of the Jewish Diaspora, where instead of historic artifacts, he found interactive displays, dioramas and videos used to illustrate various aspects of Jewish life. From this visit Kaplinski gleaned an understanding of the diversity of the Jews who had come from all corners of the world to settle in Israel. Then came the high point of his trip to the Middle East: Jerusalem.

As Kaplinski entered the Old City, the grand scale of Jerusalem's three-

Oh Jerusalem, Oh Jerusalem, **plein-air watercolor, 11" x 14" 1984. Collection of Mark Ottesen.**

thousand-year history had the same mind-boggling effect on him as had Alaska's glaciers. Events and monuments of spiritual significance make this a holy city and a place of world pilgrimage for Jews, Christians and Moslems. Here in 1000 BC David captured the city from the Canaanites; Solomon built the Temple and created the Hebrew political and spiritual capital; Christ was crucified; Mohammed visited; Crusaders fought as Christians and Muslims vied for power; the Mamluk, then Ottoman Empires ruled. Astounded that so much history could be contained within an area the size of Chicago's Maxwell Street neighborhood, Kaplinski set up his easel and worked to grapple with the Old City's immensity before taking on its individual monuments.

The complexity of Jerusalem with its parapeted walls embracing within a maze of domes, steeples, and towers of churches, temples, mosques, monasteries, and synagogues, amid a sea of homes, offices, businesses and squares, presents a difficult task for the artist. Where does he begin? How does he hope to reduce such a scene within the borders of an 11 x 14 inch paper or board, and convince the viewer that he is seeing the same busy landscape which challenged the artist?

Kaplinski's *Oh Jerusalem, Oh Jerusalem,* a plein-air watercolor of that dimension, is convincing, and on close examination the skills of the artist are bared. The crisp lines and bold warm colors in the foreground gradually yield to softer lines and cooler tones to a point where only the barest hints of structures rest on a violet horizon, forcing the eye to clearly recognize what is close while accepting only an impression of what is distant.

Once he had grasped the overall character of the Old City, Kaplinski wandered its streets, taking in the sights. He marveled at one of Islam's greatest architectural achievements, the Dome of the Rock, built in 688-691 AD in today's Muslim Quarter; he visited the Western Wall (Wailing Wall), Judaism's holiest site dating back to Herod the Great in 20 BC, in the Jewish Quarter; and then wandered up the Via Doloroso (Way of Sorrows) tracing the traditional steps of Christ from the place of his trial, to Calvary, and then to his tomb in the Church of the Holy Sepulchre in the Christian Quarter. He went outside the city gates to the Mount of Olives, known best as the site of the Agony of Christ, his betrayal in the Garden of Gethsemane, and his Ascension into Heaven.

Then Kaplinski ventured out of Jerusalem to sites important to Christ's life: Tiberias on the Sea of Galilee, where Jesus had his public ministry; to Nazareth, the site of the Annunciation; on to Capernaum, and other biblical sites—Megiddo, Masada, Beersheba and the plains of Jezreel. Returning to Jerusalem, he retraced his steps, visiting its special places for a second time, made a side trip to Bethlehem to see the Church of the Nativity, before boarding a plane back to Tel Aviv. As the sun set over the Mediterranean Sea, Kaplinski reflected on his trip. The reality of what he had seen and done in two short but intense months now became memories, recorded for posterity in his paintings. No sorrows spawned in generations past and terror of the present surface in his work—only hope, represented by the rich gold tones of the Dome of the Rock, resting on its blue and white subtending walls, dominating the walled

Old City. That seemed a fitting end to his odyssey to the Middle East.

Back in Colorado, critics took note of this new body of works, and the stylistic growth evident in his paintings of the Middle East. "Two of his most dramatic paintings, 'Oh Jerusalem, Oh Jerusalem' and 'Luxor Temple/Night-time Illumination,' underscore his skill at capturing intense light and color. The former, with the glistening Dome of the Rock near the center, contrasts hot/yellow light on building with cool/green of trees and shrubs in the foreground. The latter, with its deep purple/black sky outlining illuminated features of the Luxor Temple, is almost too extreme in its contrasts. . . . Two small paintings that warrant attention are his 'Rock Wall at Petra,' virtually abstract in its color patterns, and 'Nile Sunset,' particularly compelling in its rendering of a yellow/orange sunset (with boat) on water." [2]

Kaplinski mastered these techniques working in the American South-west, creating an illusion of the enormous expanse of desert, prairie, and mountains in a two-dimensional surface. Addressing detail became an editorial decision. The same rules are convincingly applied whether the landscape is dominated by man-made structures or is one largely untouched. His interpretation of the latter would soon be tested in the South Pacific.

CHAPTER **11**

HUMAN HASH WITH KAVA-KAVA CHASERS – AND OTHER HAZARDS IN THE SOUTH PACIFIC

With two Fijian sailing canoes in hot pursuit, only a dying wind allowed Lt. William Bligh, the castaway captain of *H.M.S. Bounty* and 18 of his officers to escape certain death. Straining at the six pairs of oars—every stroke up the crest of each wave made as if their lives depended on it—Bligh's oarsmen inched their 23-foot launch beyond the immediate reach of the pursuing cannibals.

Their escape route forced them to traverse the skein of the Fiji Islands. Until this moment in 1789, the islands were largely unknown to Europeans, although reports of cannibalism had filtered back to England—a grim reminder to remain on course.

With one eye peeled for Fijians and another through his sextant, Bligh accurately plotted their location as they brushed by the lush islands. Mapping, however, was not on the minds of the crew. Escape from this archipelago of terror, whose inhabitants held an insatiable appetite for human hash, whetted by the chase or through the clubbing of survivors of coral reef shipwrecks, drove Bligh's crew to near exhaustion. They made it. None was eaten. Bligh directed their course to refuge in Timor, the closest European outpost 3500 miles to the northwest. [1]

One hundred years later, Paul Gauguin, the French Impressionist, made his escape to the South Pacific, leaving behind a meager existence in Paris. In Tahiti he spent the last twelve years of his life struggling for acceptance of his work emphasizing plaintive features of natives, painted with soft tropical colors—far out of place in his native France. [2]

Gauguin's passage to Tahiti, during which passengers on the French superannuated sailing ship *Vire* had little inclination to rush to their berths below deck where they attempted to ignore crawling sounds in the night and acclimate to a prevailing stench of foul air, had much in common with Kaplinski's passage among the Fiji islands almost another 100 years later.

While not losing sight of the adventure which awaits, we need to pause in this last centurial leap in history to share the Kaplinskis' visits—some solo, some together—to other Polynesian regions. These also play an important part in Kaplinski's artistic development.

For years Vicky had nurtured a dream of a trip to the South Seas and

Majestic Palms of Moorea, **plein-air watercolor, 9½" x 7½" 1971. Private collection. (opposite page)**

was now hitched to a man who gave any dream an opportunity to flourish. In the late 1970s her dream became reality with Kaplinski in Bora Bora and would soon include Tahiti, Moorea, Huahine, and Raiatea.

Cascading water in Tahiti caught on camera.

On these islands, Kaplinski had to tackle colors and subjects entirely new to him. Making adjustments to his palette in order to capture the vivid colors of the South Seas, he succeeded in painting his first ever ocean-going ship. What enchanted him, however, was the flora. In this island paradise, Mother Nature abandoned all restraint and offered with a profusion of tropical plants. Flowers Kaplinski had never set eyes on before matched their exotic names: red torch ginger, flamingo flower, and Tahitian vanilla. The colors, just as vivid, ranged from the snowy white of the famed Tahitian *tiare* gardenia to the yellows of the *purau*, or Polynesian hibiscus, to the multicolored paper flowers, tissue-thin gems spanning the spectrum from beige to pale pink, fuchsia to purple, to varied hues of orange. How would he possibly capture them and the equally daunting greens of their foliage, or the leaves of a banana plant? The greens provided a frustration almost equal to the moisture of the tropical sea air and the islands' rainforested interior. It took forever for paint to dry.

Tuned in to the natural beauty of the South Pacific, Kaplinski made a solo painting trip before returning to another South Sea island group with Vicky. In 1982 he packed his hiking boots, camera and painting gear for an

Waterfall, Tahiti, acrylic, 10" x 8" 1976. Private Collection. Kaplinski departs from the cool gray and violate hues of the rock and cascading water emphasized by the camera (opposite page) and warms the scene with earth tones. His treatment provides some chromatic relief from the piercing blue-white of the water without compromising the energy of this enchanting Tahitian scene.

intensive study of New Zealand's glaciers and fiords. Auckand offered an introduction to the "pristine country where people spoke English, had tea and crumpets, and drove on the wrong side of the road." After painting the bustling seaport wih its bridges and two magnificent harbors, Kaplinski set his brushes to work on the indigenous beech trees, the nikau palm and the giant coniferous kauri tree unique to the subtropical North Island.

Kaplinski briefly paid homage to Christchurch, New Zealand's oldest city established by Royal Charter in 1856, and in his opinion, the most English city in New Zealand; then arrived at his first destination, Mount Cook National Park, located in the heart of the South Island's Southern Alps. In this wilderness landscape, glaciers cover forty percent of the park's terrain. Rugged mountains, including twenty-two of New Zealand's twenty-seven peaks over 10,000 feet high, make up the rest of the territory. Crowning the South Alps is Mount Cook, New Zealand's highest mountain, sacred to the Maori. Its 12,349-foot stature earned it the name "Aoraki," a Maori word meaning "cloud piercer." Besides Mount Cook, its pinnacle hidden in the clouds, Kaplinski

Kaplinski on Brampton Reef – North Island, New Zealand.

painted some of the numerous waterfalls spilling down towering cliffs.

From the inland maze of mountains, Kaplinski traveled west to the South Island's second and largest national park, Fiordland. Fourteen fiords serrate the rugged 124 miles of the park's mountainous coastline, where millions of years ago glaciers scoured the landscape. Kaplinski spent time in the famed Milford Sound to the north, entranced by the rainforest and the water. In the park's "most exquisite spot," he painted drizzly landscapes along the fiord's ten-mile stretch. He thought the mangrove trees, depicted in his painting of Milford Sound, had a lot of character. The landscape reminded him of scenes from *Tarzan and the Apes.* By its very majesty, Milford Sound's best-known landmark, Mitre Peak, merited attention from Kaplinski's brush. The pyramid-shaped mountain, resembling a bishop's miter, rises a dramatic 5,500 feet into the air out of the depths of the fiord.

Mangrove Tree At Low Tide, Brampton Reef – North Island, New Zealand, **watercolor, 11" x 14". Collection of Sue Soder. Kaplinski has enriched the hints of color as he must have detected them on site and captured by the camera (previous page). The tree's dominance and drama are achieved by its separation from the surrounding rocky shore through the inlet of water in the foreground.**

The Cloud Piercer – Aorangi, New Zealand, acrylic on canvas, 24" x 36" 1992.

After painting in the rainforests of New Zealand, Kaplinski developed an enthusiasm for the brilliant orchids, birds of paradise, and other island flora of Hawaii. These flowers found their way into a number of colorful and representational still lifes. In some paintings, the artist gives each species center stage: in one the orange, stork-like head of a bird of paradise hangs suspended on a white backdrop; in another pink plumeria blossoms play against their green. Then a riot of flowers—red anthurium, pale pink plumeria, fuchsia hibiscus, orange-and-purple bird of paradise and a huge white anthurium—set against a green jungle of bamboo with a waterfall pounding spray in the background appear in *Hawaiian Flower Fantasy*. Yet, for all the color and detail in these paintings, complete satisfaction with the series had eluded him. Although stylishly done, Kaplinski felt he had exhausted the nuances of these tropical beauties. He had, however, not encountered them all. His show, *The Spell of Hawaii*, held at Hilo's Mauna Kea hotel in 1987, opened a new horizon for Kaplinski and Vicky who had joined him in Hawaii. "There's only

Milford Sound – Fiordland, New Zealand,
**acrylic on canvas, 30" x 40"
1992. Collection of Steve "Grizzly"
Adams.**

one place you can find them in any significant numbers," a patron informed Kaplinski. "In Taveuni the rare tangimauthia hangs in red-and-white sleigh-bell clusters, and you'll be so caught up in the beauty of the place, you'll forget to paint them!" Not only was the subject of the suggested quest intriguing to Kaplinski, its location had the making of adventure. A sense of foreboding stirred in Vicky.

From Suva in the heart of the Fiji islands they flew to Taveuni, Fiji's "Garden Island." By now Kaplinski had mastered the colors of the tropics, his hues as vibrant as Gauguin's. His anticipation to do justice to the tangimau-thia's legendary red-and-white cascading clusters grew as the plane haltingly braked to a stop on the tarmac.

The Kaplinskis quickly arranged transportation to the mountain forests surrounding a crater lake among the extinct volcanoes, expecting to be guided to their objective by the usual hovering mists above them. To their dismay the forests appeared to lose their foliage as they neared, and it became apparent that some recent disaster had struck. A typhoon had stripped away all but the sturdiest leaf and flower. Even the jungle sounds had been blown away. Not much to paint. Not a sound to be remembered.

One hardy, untouched survivor was the pepper plant from which Fijians for centuries have concocted kava-kava, a potent intoxicating drink. The first Europeans to savor it were possibly the early 19th century sandalwood traders who eventually ripped every stick of the precious wood from Fiji to meet the insatiable commercial demands of the Chinese. Seated ceremoniously on pandanus mats in the presence of their ostensibly friendly Fijian hosts, the pungent kava-kava perhaps lessened these traders' concern that they would fall victim to a war club and be served up as the main course.

Discouraged, Buffalo and Vicky headed back towards the port, and as they neared the coast slowed the car upon entering a small village. Before them was a group of woven-roofed houses and a few men in traditional *sulus*, a skirt that looks remarkably stylish when paired with white long-sleeved shirts with rolled-up sleeves.

Kaplinski attracted his usual coterie of onlookers as his sable brush recreated the soft roof lines of the pandanus-thatched huts and angled trunks of palm trees whose branches cast dancing shadows on the roofs and sides of these traditional structures. Satisfied with this intimate scene, Kaplinski packed up his paints and brushes and he and Vicky continued their descent.

Their adventure then took another turn for the worse. The hotel recommended in their guidebook was all boarded up. Friendly Fijians for the moment, saved the situation. The Kaplinskis met a native woman who offered to rent them her large beach house, complete with electricity, ants and night-crawling insects. That night, finding no good meals on the island, they also had bad luck with the weather. It had turned foul. The next morning Vicky happened to look out the window into the rain and wind. She was alarmed to see flying objects—an easel, a pad of paper, a palette box and paintbrushes—and rushed outside to find Kaplinski raging and railing. "I can't paint in this," he thundered.

He stormed off in search of a boat to transport them back to Viti Levu,

Hawaiian Flower Fantasy, **watercolor, 30" x 22" 1987. Collection of Mr. and Mrs. Juan Dimas. (opposite page)**

and returned to tell Vicky the good news. He'd found a boat that would leave at noon the next day. At the appointed time, they boarded a multi-decked ferry. Assorted domestic animals were led below, and the human cargo consisted of native Fijians, East Indian immigrants whose ancestors most likely had been brought to Fiji to work the copra plantations, and a handful of tourists. Unmindful of distances in the South Pacific or of the speed of the ferry which was to transport them to the island of Viti Levu to the west of Taveuni, they anticipated a trip of less than a day. "You'll arrive at 4:00 in the afternoon," the ticket agent chirped assuredly.

The Kaplinskis located one of the few open areas on the upper deck, and as the ferry shuddered in reverse pulling away from the dock, a soft South Pacific breeze welcomed them to the route where for centuries Fijians had traveled from island to island. Four o'clock came, went, and the only islands in sight were those left behind. The smell of curry disguising the mysteries of some questionable ingredients competed with the odors of assorted animals stabled below protesting their confinement in every way nature provides. Vicky hadn't gotten the hang of eating greasy Indian food with her hands, and each time the vessel stopped to take on more passengers, the sanitation level in the lavatories dropped. To cap it off, the stench of diesel exhaust fell heavily on the decks in the waning late-afternoon breeze, prompting Kaplinski to approach one of the ship's officers asking what had delayed their arrival.

"What delay? We're right on schedule," he replied. "By four o'clock tomorrow afternoon we'll be well within sight of Viti Levu!"

This news would not settle well with Vicky, whose enjoyment of a daytime voyage was already stretched to the limit. Overnight she might recall some other adventures with her husband from which she had found an escape. Here that was impossible.

From a wooden bench set against a steel bulkhead, they watched the sun dip below the horizon. The lingering luscious red lining of the few clouds suspended above and the muted rumble of the ship's engine below were abruptly replaced by a piercing blue-white glare and garbled voices from a video monitor in the main cabin. Eventually the ship quieted down, exhaustion took hold, and the Kaplinskis huddled together, waiting for night to pass. On schedule the following day, the ferry squeezed into its berth at Suva. Nobody lingered aboard.

The Kaplinskis decided to finish their trip in style, and secluded themselves in a resort area on the Coral Coast. After their devastating experience in Taveuni, they had earned some enjoyment. Ignoring advertisements for a boat tour through *lomalagi*, or paradise, they departed from Fiji. As they circled over Vitu Levi, their plane banked to the left, treating them to the last rays of an orange setting sun reaching toward them—perhaps an invitation to return. Unlike Gauguin, Kaplinski chose not to accept. No tropical studio, like Gauguin's, has been attempted. Yet Kaplinski's visits to the South Pacific exposed him to new light, color, people, and customs, and instilled a desire— although it would take some years for the memories of his Fijian disaster to fade—for another foreign adventure.

CHAPTER 12 SPAIN'S HANGING HOUSES AND MOROCCAN SOUKS

Gearing up for their trip to Spain and Morocco in 1993, Kaplinski and Vicky worked their way through guidebooks and historic texts targeting cities and regions most likely to reflect the character of the people and their country. "King Juan Carlos and Queen Sofia haven't invited us for dinner," Buffalo chided Vicky as they stared at the bulging suitcases laid out on the floor of their ranch in Elizabeth. "If we need something special to wear, put it on the credit card not in the suitcase!"

Kaplinski had envisioned aristocrats at lunch—impeccably dressed—along the Gran Via, Madrid's Broadway, and Francisco Goya's eighteenth-century palette of human faces: gypsies, idlers, lovers, and street musicians. The palette of his imagination changed when he and Vicky landed in Madrid. The Kaplinskis took in Madrid's dizzying assortment of buildings—palaces, convents, museums, and churches—that had blossomed under the patronage of Philip II, who moved the Spanish court there in 1561. They wandered through the Old City, with the imposing Plaza Mayor at its heart, through mazes of narrow streets and its mini-neighborhoods with plazas of their own. From the old city center, they emerged onto grand boulevards lined with stately neoclassical buildings. Once acclimated to Spain's capital, they visited the museum devoted to Joaquin Sorolla, the famous Spanish "painter of light." This mission completed, they headed south into the country's heartland.

Kaplinski first wet his brushes in Toledo, perched high on a hill overlooking the Río Rajo. He found the smaller city and the surrounding countryside more to his liking. Predominating as a center of Muslim scholarship and arts, Toledo was central Spain's main Moorish city in the eleventh century. The Old City, immortalized on canvas by El Greco and adopted as his home in the late 1570s, showed little change. Kaplinski was entranced with the magnificent Cathedral of Toledo, built between the thirteenth and fifteenth centuries, the city's most impressive example of Gothic architecture. Moving on to Segovia, in the once mighty Christian center of Castile, Kaplinski found the

Moroccan Souk. **Drawing by Buffalo Kaplinski.**

Roman aqueduct, a marvel of engineering, and the famous Alcazar Castle equally impressive.

As in Greece, Kaplinski's paintings of Spain often focused on the architecture of the regions he visited. South of Madrid in the Castilla-La Mancha province, Cuenca's medieval hanging houses, bearing the patina of time and projecting over the Júcar River, lose little of their dizzying impact in Kaplinski's watercolors. Once senses that the collapse of Italy's medieval equivalent, Civita di Bagnoregio, could here repeat itself at any moment. The sight of Cuenca, the panorama of buildings clinging precariously to cliff edges, vines and trees turning changing summer colors for those of autumn, all set on a beige mesa, set Kaplinski's artistic senses spinning. " I look at this gold mine of subjects and Vicky agrees, I can paint, if only for an afternoon—

Hanging Houses of Cuenca, **watercolor, 26" x 19" 1993. Collection of Mr. and Mrs. Robert Vogel.**

I do so but only by dodging raindrops and tourists." [1] An ordinary approach to such a scene would be to emphasize the red roofs and sharp contrasts with cliffs and building exteriors. Yet Kaplinski made full use of reflected light which provides a colorful anchor to the houses beyond.

North of Madrid in Old Castile, the city of Burgos, once a center of trade, was Spain's prestigious capital city until the 1560s when Philip II declared Madrid the *única corte* or only court. The cathedral in Burgos, founded in 1221 by Ferdinand III of Castile and completed in 1567, a fine example of florid Gothic, inspired Kaplinski's brushes. Painting its complexities, always

Cathedral at Burgos, **watercolor, 20"
x 28" 1993. Collection of Tim and
Christina Fritschel.**

a challenge to the artist to simplify while simultaneously teasing the viewer
into believing in its grandeur, was even more difficult in the unrelenting rain.
Although the rain added an element of mystery, Kaplinski had to abandon
plein-air efforts. His *Cathedral at Burgos,* was created later as a studio piece.
Inside the cathedral, he paid his respects to the chivalrous eleventh-century
knight, Rodrigo Díaz de Vivar, better known as El Cid, buried there with his
wife, Jimena. Then he headed south with Vicky to La Mancha.

There is a Spanish saying that "The Andalusian sings, the Extremaduran
fights, and the Castilian dreams." Among the Castilian dreamers, the greatest
of all, Don Quixote, from La Mancha, best exemplifies that temperament.
The same wind that turned the arms of the "monstrous giants" invoking Quixote's charge and cry, "Fly not cowards. . . ," slowly turned the blades of six
windmills atop a hill in Campo de Criptana, inviting paper and brush from

Zahara, Spain, watercolor, 22" x 30"
**1993. Collection of John and Lynn
Fritschel.**

Kaplinski's art box. He saw no pure white in the whitewashed stone windmill houses—rather violets, blues, and grays complementing the sky behind and above, accented by bold trim colors around doors and windows.

From La Mancha the Kaplinskis traversed the tablelands of Extremadura, homeland to Spanish conquistadors, Francisco Pizarro and Hernán Cortés, en route to Andalucia's Ruta Pueblo Blancos (Route of White Villages). Among the rugged hills of the Sierra de Cádiz, fortified villages, once on the frontier between Moorish and Christian kingdoms, line the edges of deep, river-carved gorges, strung out like a rope of white pearls. Kaplinski recalled his initial impressions: "This part of Spain is especially picturesque and looks like that picture postcard somebody sent you from Spain. Very sunny and the whitewashed towns radiate light—hurting your eyes." While staying at the Government *parador* (hotel), the Kaplinskis used the picturesque village of Arcos de la Frontera, perched high above the Río Guadalete, as home base for

Kaplinski at Zahara, Spain. The town appears to be separated from the dominant geologic structure that must have originally drawn its inhabitants to settle there. In his painting of Zahara (previous page) Kaplinski has rearranged the topography and comfortably nestled the houses within the protective shadow of the hillside. The town seems to rise from the rubble that fell from the fractured mountain. Kaplinski has emphasized the blue and violet hues, which the camera has missed.

visiting other villages on the route. Kaplinski soon found his way to Zahara, an ancient Moorish outpost on his "must paint" list. Its impregnable Moorish castle, built in the tenth century, lent strategic importance to this stunning mountain village. Today Zahara overlooks the Garganta Seca, a huge reservoir, and the valley spreading below. As evident in Kaplinski's *Zahara, Spain,* the lightheartedness of the Andalusian people and their sunny, whitewashed towns permeates his landscapes, without ever being repetitive.

Leaving the route of white washed villages, the Kaplinskis traveled to Ronda, one of Andalucía's most picturesque towns. Originally a Moorish stronghold, the Old Town is replete with ancient churches, palaces and monuments testifying to its rich history. There Kaplinski found the town's remarkable *Puente Nuevo,* an amazing feat of engineering built in the eighteenth century, poised high atop two six-hundred-foot cliffs and straddling the deep El Tajo gorge—just the kind of dramatic landscape he liked to paint. He did an on-the-spot watercolor from a worm's eye view. The vantage point he selected showcases whitewashed buildings seen through the bridge's keyhole arch, set against a brilliant blue sky. Billowing white clouds echo and accent the dazzling sunlit structures.

Venturing deeper into Andalucia, the couple found ocean cottages for rent just outside Marabella on the Costa del Sol. Kaplinski ventured off to paint the boats, fishermen and their nets in the fishing villages of Estopona and Nerja. "Holy mackerel," he later said. "The harbor there was fantastic . . . loaded to the gills with tremendous subjects." [2] Pausing for some relaxation east of Gilbraltar on the Mediterranean Sea, the Kaplinskis gave further thought to the next leg of their journey: Morocco. The mysteries of Morocco's colorful *souks* or marketplaces, casbahs, camels, and desert seemed so distant from the pristine beaches and soft Mediterranean breezes of the Costa del Sol. Yet Ned Jacob's repeated urgings over the past year or two, and recollections of his oils and charcoal drawings of camel markets and turbaned Berbers, provided the incentive for this venture. Departing from Spain's port city of Algeciras, they were ferried across to Morocco. Their two-and-a-half-hour crossing of the Strait of Gilbraltar ended at the port city of Tangier. As soon as they landed, the chorus began.

Bridge at Rhonda, **plein-air watercolor, 15½" x 12½" 1993. Collection of Mr. and Mrs. Tom Lord.**

"Do you need a hotel?"

"No."

"My brother works at a clean Hotel."

"No!"

"It is very cheap, Sir. Perhaps you need to change money?"

"No, thanks."

Once settled in their hotel, Kaplinski escaped the pesky hucksters to paint Tangier's harbor and the ancient walled town of Asila on cliffs above the

Can You Fix It Mohammed?, watercolor, 16" x 20" 1993. Collection of Bill and Adelaide Murray.

Atlantic Ocean, where views from the ramparts overlook mighty waves crashing on the rocks below. Returning to Tangier, he and Vicky experienced some of the port city's local color when they visited the Souk el Arba Ayacha. By now the two of them had come to grips with culture shock and were ready to venture into Morocco's interior.

The train to Fes, Morocco's cultural capital, provided welcome relief from the street hustlers of Tangier. The only worry the Kaplinskis had was how they would get around in the ancient city. They didn't read or speak Arabic and the guidebooks had all stated that a guide was necessary in Fes to avoid becoming hopelessly lost in the maze of the ancient city's streets. Providence intervened in the guise of Abdelali, a guitar teacher in Fes, whom they met on the train. Abdelali lived in the oldest part of Fes, an enclave founded in 808 AD and continuously inhabited since that time, and knew its every twist and turn. He proved to be a welcome friend and guide as he introduced the Kaplinskis to his city. Most importantly, he sensed needs of the visual artist: locating interesting subject matter, and finding a place to paint without interruption. Like Mohammed Ahmeol Abed, Kaplinski's guide in Luxor, Abdelali stood guard while Kaplinski explored, photographed and worked at his easel.

The sights, smells, and sounds of Morocco's *souks* are as challenging for the visitor to absorb as it is for the artist

Bab Fatouch – Fes, acrylic on canvas, 10½" x 10½". Collection of the artist.

to record. Where to begin? Nothing seems to fit. The cry, *balek, balek!*—"make way, make way!"—is repeated throughout the market. Donkeys loaded with strange merchandise force those walking along the narrow streets to flatten into doorways to allow the beasts to pass; a heady mixture of thyme, orange, bay leaf, saffron, and mint fill the air; and the clutter of copperware of all sizes and shapes for purposes largely unknown to the visitor, reflect sun by day and strange iridescence at night. Archaic scales, themselves a step back in time, weigh the burdens of the day as much as the grains, leaves, and powders sold by the vendors.

Here, complexity of architecture is enhanced by the dissonance of the market and identifying a manageable subject requires selectivity. Kaplinski chose the copperware vendors and the clutter of culinary paraphernalia. The brass and copper and their reflected light offer almost a cathedral-like backdrop for the congregation of dishes, bowls, and kettles.

Keyhole arches in the heart of Fes tested Kaplinski's concentration when surrounded with the bustle of the foot traffic while executing the sweeping lines of the arches before him. One watercolor of this traditional structure employed soft background lighting, inviting the eye to move easily from the architectural details of the structures to the cityscape in the distance.

Through Abdelali's hospitality, the Kaplinskis had entrée to a more in-depth experience in Morocco. He invited them to breakfast at his home, where they met his family, and he also joined them for lunch. On their last night in Fes, Abdelali took Kaplinski deep into the Casbah, past the Mausoleum of Moulay Idress II (the city's founder), past the Kaiwine Mosque, down narrow pathways and hallways, through an abyss of ancient adobe, stone and mosaics. On this night the artist experienced the true spell of Fes. The next morning, Abdelali appeared at the train station to bid the Kaplinskis farewell. They said goodbye, hoping to see each other again—*Inchalla*—if it is God's will. After their experience with the street hustlers of Tangier, they were relieved to know someone in Morocco who simply wanted to be friends. Back in Tangier, they returned to Hotel Rembrandt (where else would an artist stay?) and left to resume their Spanish adventure the next day.

Their sidetrip to Fes helped prepare the Kaplinskis for their next stop: Granada. Considered by some Spain's finest city, it was the seat and final strong-hold of Moorish Spain, until 1492 when it fell to the Spanish Roman Catholic monarchs Ferdinand II and Isabella I. Rife with notable buildings—churches ranging in style from Gothic to Neoclassical, including Santa María de la En-carnación (1523-1703) with its Capilla Real (Royal Chapel) containing the tombs of Ferdinand and Isabella,—and various monasteries, palaces and man-sions, Granada's "dazzler" in Kaplinski's mind was the famed Alhambra, one of the great accomplishments of Islamic architecture. Contained within its walls are the Alcazaba, the fortress occupied by the Moors from the eleventh through the thirteenth centuries; the Palacio Nazaries (Nasrid Palace), the Alhambra's centerpiece, where Muslim rulers lived; and the Generalife palace gardens. The extensive gardens and the sublime structures reached beyond Kaplinski's wild-est expectations. "The whole concept is a compliment to the ingenuity of the Arabs who built this in 1238," he later wrote. [3]

On this high note, the Kaplinskis set off for Barcelona, their final desti-

Alhambra Fantasia, watercolor, 19" x 15" 1996.
(opposite page)

nation. In Cataluña's capital, they turned in their car. Kaplinski packed up all his art supplies, and played tourist with Vicky. They strolled together from the Plaça de Cataluña, Barcelona's central plaza down the huge tree-lined boulevard, La Rambla. The famed street provides a never-ending bustle of activity with its open-air markets, kiosks and newsstands, bird and flower stalls, restaurants and cafés.

Of all the sights, probably the chimerical creations of architect Antoni Gaudí, leading exponent of *Modernisme* or the Spanish style of Art Nouveau, made the deepest impression. The architect worked on his life masterpiece, *La Sagrada Família* (Church of the Holy Family), for over forty years, from 1883 until his death in 1926. The resulting church is a unique mixture of *Modernista* elements combined with aspects of Gothic architecture, seen particularly in its eight three-hundred-foot-high bell towers. Gaudí's blending decorative elements—the figures of saints, musicians, angels and animals—directly into the church's exterior façade, caused Monsignor Ragonesi, Papal Nuncio in Spain, on a visit in 1915 to call the maestro "the Dante of architecture." Vicky reacted most strongly to Gaudí's avant-garde, nearly surrealistic design style. She remembered, at first assessment, thinking that the architect was nuts. After the magnificence of structures like the Alhambra, his strange works seemed out of place; the kind of art "that had to grow on you." [4]

On their last night in Spain, the Kaplinskis joined the constant stream of fellow promenaders on La Rambla. After taking advantage of an abundance of people-watching opportunities, they retired, exhausted and happy, to their hotel.

In the span of five weeks, Kaplinski had completed thirty paintings on location. Once back home, he balanced the number with larger and more complex studio works. With his works of Spain and Morocco, Kaplinski renewed the interest of his Colorado patrons. They welcomed him back. He made his first Denver gallery appearance in ten years. In May 1994 Denver's Opicka Gallery hosted the exhibition entitled *Spanish Treasures and Moroccan Mosaics*. In the gallery brochure, Kaplinski remarked that, besides challenging him with a myriad of new and wondrous subjects, his trip to Spain and Morocco resulted in his greatest growth in years.

Eager to continue his quest to find ever-new challenges, he considered where to go next. His adventures along the Mediterranean had taken him to southern Europe and to areas around the Middle East. He had traveled to island groups in the South Pacific. Painting in these regions had expanded Kaplinski's horizons and capabilities beyond the by-now-familiar Colorado and other western states. Perhaps he would now seek out a more northern clime; a place where he would find different color and light; somewhere rich with architecture, like Spain and Greece, but with different atmospheric conditions; maybe somewhere where he could get around more easily speaking his native tongue. Within a year he had found just the place.

CHAPTER 13 CROWN JEWEL LANDSCAPES OF ENGLAND AND SCOTLAND

Charles Dickens' unsinkable character, Wilkins Micawber boldly announced: "I am . . . delighted to add that I have now an immediate prospect of something turning up." Whether it be Dickensian phrases, the soft, silvery stone of Canterbury Cathedral, mottled fields blanketing the rolling Cotswolds hills, Bath's graceful stone houses formed in crescents and squares, and soft light unlike the brilliance of the American Southwest or Greece, Kaplinski anticipated in 1995 that something good would surely turn up in England and Scotland.

London gave Kaplinski a taste of England's painting prospects that would follow. He spent "three days of amazement" exploring the city's architecture steeped in history. He climbed the Tower Bridge, built in 1677 to commemorate the Great Fire of London, for a bird's eye view of the city and its monuments. Returning to ground level, Kaplinski visited the Houses of Parliament, contained within the "new" Palace of Westminster, built on the site King Henry VIII's former residence; and London's famous timepiece, towering 300 feet above the Westminster complex, Big Ben, named after the immense, nearly fourteen-ton bell that strikes the hour. Forsaking architecture for the famed British gardens, Kaplinski prepared to wander some of Kew Gardens' three hundred acres. Like thousands of other visitors, he enjoyed the many greenhouses, including the distinctive nineteenth-century curved glass Palm House, and strolling along grounds designed by master English landscape gardener, Capability Brown. After seeing this Royal Botanic gem, he left London for Oxford.

Victorian poet Mathew Arnold had termed Oxford a "city of dreaming spires" to describe its exquisite skyline of towers and steeples. Once a Saxon fording point for oxen, Oxford later became a *burg* to defend England's northern frontier from Danish attack. Little remains of the Saxon settlement, which today is best known for the University of Oxford's complex of buildings. Among these famed structures, dating primarily from the fifteenth, sixteenth, and seventeenth centuries, Christ Church received the most notoriety in literature

York, U.K. **Drawing by Buffalo Kaplinski.**

Chocolate Box House, Cotswolds, U.K.,
plein-air watercolor, 16"x 24".
Collection of Jean Chrest.

and film. Lewis Carroll used the college as the setting for *Alice in Wonderland*, and Evelyn Waugh set his novel, *Brideshead Revisited*, there; most recently Christ Church appeared on film in the Harry Potter movie series. Oxford provided Kaplinski with a "feast of architecture" that also included the old Ashmolean Museum, designed by architect Christopher Wren and built in the latter 1600s; and the Clarendon Building, built in the early 1700s by Wren's greatest pupil, Nicholas Hawksmoor, to house the original printing operations of the Oxford University Press. As well known as some of the authors with connections to Oxford—J.R.R. Tolkien, C. S. Lewis, and Iris Murdoch—might be, none match the fame of Shakespeare.

Although one of the seven properties associated with the Bard's life, Anne Hathaway's Cottage, merited Kaplinski's attention, he found lesser known dwellings equally attractive. He delighted the owner of the B & B,

Ley's View Cottage, Slaughter, Cotswolds,
**plein-air watercolor, 15½" x 11½"
1996. Collection of Mr. and Mrs. Jack
Richeson.**

where he comfortably resided in Stratford-upon-Avon, with a picture emphasizing its sloping thatched roof, brick chimneys, low doors, and small-paned windows—typical of Cotswolds cottages—and primroses, as common to the English garden as hollyhocks are to northern New Mexico. "Why, it's our Chocolate Box House!" he exclaimed, proudly referring to his modest home shared with travelers. "Of course, luv," his beaming wife added, suggesting in her tone that their humble quarters ranked with castles and cathedrals in the artist's eye.

After the architectural grandeur of London and Oxford, Kaplinski now focused on the famous stone cottages of the Cotswolds, the region considered the "heart of England." The area's yellow limestone, hand-hewn to build Roman settlements and Saxon villages, helped create a harmonious mosaic of attractive towns, woods and farmlands. Grazing on the rich green grasses that flourish on limestone, sheep and cattle, alongside the stone "cots," dot undulating pastureland outlined by honey-colored stone walls. These elements make up the distinctive character of one of England's finest landscapes—special enough to earn Cotswold Hills the designation: Area of Outstanding National Beauty, England's

Anne Hathaway's Cottage, **plein-air watercolor, 10½" x 13" 1996. Collection of Jack Richeson.**

equivalent of a National Park, in 1966.

Drawn to the reputedly "more picturesque" area, Kaplinski chose to paint the Northern Cotswolds. Headquartered in Stow-on-the-Wold, he made day-trips to nearby villages with names as enchanting as the landscape—Bourton-on-the-Water, Windrush, Little Rollright, Welford-upon-Avon. The most striking of these villages (after Stratford-upon-Avon, of course) was Chipping Camden, one of the richest wool towns of England. The town's long High Street, lined with sixteenth-century stone houses lead to the striking Church of St. James. Built in the Perpendicular style in the fifteenth century, like many other churches in the region, it attests to Cotwold's booming wool trade in the Middle Ages. Chipping Camden enjoys a larger reputation as the home of the Arts and Crafts movement, founded in the early twentieth century by William Morris.

The Rows at Chester, Bridge Street and Eastgate, plein-air watercolor, 15½" x 11½" 1996. Collection of Mr. and Mrs. Doug Phillips.

Kaplinski had no lack of subject matter, just time. Mindful of his itinerary, he took a train from Coventry to Chester, the city with a history as colorful as its architecture. With origins as a Roman legion's fortress site, the town Deva (ca. 70 AD), with its massive harbour and strategic border position, became a major trading port until the Romans withdrew in the fifth century AD. By 900 Danish and Saxon marauders had nearly decimated the town. Its revival began under the Normans around 1070, and by the Middle Ages, Chester had regained its stature as a center of shipping trade. During this time of prosperity, construction began on buildings like the famous Rows, built in the thirteenth century, which attracted Kaplinski's attention. He was dazzled by their Tudor "Magpie" architecture.

The Elizabethan elegance of plaster and black oak half-timbered buildings in Kaplinski's watercolor provides an example of a pictorial convention also used by British landscape painter, J.M.W. Turner. By amplifying the size of the featured architectural structure, and using relatively compact groups of people, slightly undersized, to make it appear even larger and more important, a subtle sense of the subject's grandeur is achieved. This architectural contrasting is apparent in Turner's work, *View of Salisbury Cathedral from the Bishop's Garden (c. 1798),* with its elongated tower and small cluster of people resting on the immense stretch of lawn leading to the walls of the south side of the cathedral. In *The Rows at Chester – Bridge Street and Eastgate,* Kaplinski magnifies the distinctive medieval buildings through precise attention to detail, effecting a further reduction in the size of the pedestrians below, suggested by a scant few strokes of his brush.

Like Turner, Kaplinski had a fascination with harbors set against the sea. Along the eastern coast of Yorkshire he painted the seacoast town of Whitby, where local craftsmen built the ships that carried Captain James Cook in his two circumnavigations of the globe. Whitby's prominence as a whaling port and its quaint streets brought the town literary fame. In his novel, *Moby-Dick*, Herman Melville paid homage to the captain of some of the first ships to sail to Greenland, William Scoresby; Whitby provided Bram Stoker with inspiration for *Dracula.* The town had another reputation, almost as dramatic as Count Dracula's. Like two other Kaplinski destinations, the nearby coastal villages of Straithes and Robin Hood's Bay, at one time Whitby figured heavily in the smuggling trade.

After painting the wild land of the Yorkshire Moors around the village of Goathland, Kaplinski traveled through the land of the wild, the "Borders" area in Northumberland. He painted Bamburgh Castle perched high on a basalt outcrop overlooking the turbulent North Sea. From there Kaplinski had a stunning view of the Holy Island, Lindisfarne, the next subject of his brushes. Stopping in Eyemouth to interpret its picturesque harbor, his next inspiration came from the sea cliffs and bird rookeries of St. Abbs along the Berwickshire coastline.

Eager to paint in Scotland, Kaplinski stopped for a few days in bonnie Edinburgh, sometimes called "the Athens of the North." From the capital city's architecture—Edinburgh Castle, its dark and brooding exterior crowning the other historic structures along the Royal Mile—to the natural beauty of its *gloaming* or fading sunsets, the artist found enough drama to warrant a chapter of its own. Yet he couldn't linger. He had reservations to travel the

Ben Nevis, Scotland, watercolor, 20" x 28" 1996. Collection of Sandy Dreher.

Castle at Bamburgh, plein-air watercolor, 30" x 24" 1996. Collection of Mr. and Mrs. Doug Phillips.
(opposite page)

West Highland Line over the bogs through the moors to Fort William. Always attracted to nature's superlatives, Kaplinski had to paint Ben Nevis, at 4,406 feet the highest mountain in the British Isles.

The setting, looking across the lake past the docked sailing vessels and harbor buildings to foothills culminating in the mountain's misty summit, provoked a use of color that rivaled Turner's. The British artist and Kaplinski share a mutual exuberant sense of color. A review of Turner's work in 1823, assessed his palette as an extravagance of "colouring not always to be discovered in the general appearance of nature." [1] A more considered view expressed ten years later, referring to Turner's exaggerations of color, was that the landscape "instantly becomes invested with an interest far beyond what a mere dry, though literal, transcript would possess." [2]

These same assessments can be made of Kaplinski's work, most notably of his plein-air watercolors. In his interpretation of Ben Nevis in Scotland, the sun-bathed farm buildings clustered in the foreground exaggerate the immensity of the water and mountains extending beyond. Kaplinski has added

pink and blue to the distant peaks, yet only on critical atmospheric assessment would the viewer realize that it is not the last rays of an evening sun that inspired these contrasting hues. Kaplinski divined them from hints of color he detected and aggressively exploited to invest, in the words of Turner's critics, an interest far beyond a literal transcript of the landscape.

With Fort William on Loch Linnhe as his base camp, Kaplinski could have traveled northwards to Inverness and Loch Ness. He chose to forego a glimpse of the monster, and headed west. Bound for the steep mountains and rugged scenery around Loch Shiel, he had the opportunity to paint at "sublime Glenfinnan." Kaplinski had completed his itinerary and reached the north of Scotland. Back in Colorado he recalled the end of his trip: "I was completely exhausted from painting on location and sightseeing—fully satisfied that I had indeed painted the Crown Jewel landscapes of England and Scotland."

One charm of the English countryside must forever elude the artists that strive to record the essentials of its spirit. The pealing of church bells heard faintly from adjoining villages, which have for centuries tolled England's joy and sadness, fall silent on the artist's brush. While paintings amply capture the scene, these gentle sounds must be drawn from memory.

In contrast, Kaplinski's paintings from Patagonia, visited several years later, carry their own imaginary sound track. One can sense the thunderous cracking of glacial ice and sweeping wind from his stark renderings of its peaks and glaciers. Kaplinski had no illusions about the harshness of the landscape and the extreme weather conditions, fierce winds spawning equally ferocious storms, as he planned his route through the Strait of Magellan and its northern reaches.

Exploring Patagonia via *Nao* and Paintbrush   Chapter 14

Four square-sailed Spanish ships under the command of Ferdinand Magellan fought their way south along the eastern shore of Patagonia, bludgeoned by heavy seas and lashed by hail and sleet. Their crews struggled on icy decks to keep the rigging from being stripped away while they desperately tried to hold their own in what became known as "the sea of graves."

Magellan's search for a passage through the enormous barrier of land, which had confronted him following his Atlantic crossing in 1519, was based on a presumption: No continuous coastline existed from pole to pole in the Old World, so why should the New lack a navigable passage to the Spice Islands in the west? [1]

Patagonia. **Drawing by Buffalo Kaplinski.**

As the tiny ships rounded a point of land, buffeted by headwinds, and waves as high as their masts, a magnificent bay opened before them offering relief from the raging seas and hope that *el paso* had been found. Indeed, the towering landscape to either side suggested a strait, yet the proper route through it would prove elusive. A maze of fjords, bays, and sounds tested the skills and judgment of navigators and helmsmen as they worked their way westward. At night, natives on the bank of the landmass to the southeast would light campfires which produced an eerie glow and led Magellan to name it *Tierra de los Fuegos.*

Mt. Sarmiento at 7,218 feet with its glaciers dazzling white in the periodic sunshine, forced Magellan, correctly, to the northwest and, days later, onto the *Mar Pacifico*, and out of the strait that was forever to bear his name. Today the intermittent groan of glaciers voicing objection to their laborious eternal movement in the *Magellanes*, the region Magellan sailed, brings to mind the creak of tired planks and the twisting of yardarms struggling to bear away from the cold relentless winds which drove Magellan's tiny flotilla into navigational history. [2]

The wind was up—fierce as it generally is in Strait of Magellan—as Kaplinski entered Torres del Paine National Park in southern Chile in 2003. While the weather is brutal at times and the country vast and rugged, the

The Highest Goal – Cuernos del Paine From Sendero Mirador Cuernos, **watercolor, 16½" x 25" 2003. Private collection.**

Patagonia of Chile is known for its glorious lake district. Within Chile's 935-square-mile national park, similar to Yellowstone or Yosemite in beauty and variety of ecosystems, is a pristine wonderland of lakes, waterfalls, glaciers—and mountains. The Macizo del Paine, the massif or principal mountain mass, which lies to the east of the Andes' spine, consists of granite, capped by shale and other sedimentary rocks. The erosive power of wind and rain carved the sedimentary uplifts into fantastic forms, evident in the park's most famous set of peaks, called the *Cuernos* or horns, and the *Torres*, the towers.

Kaplinski was eager to catch the first glimpse of the *Torres*, the park's namesake. The three granite towers, the loftiest of which rises to 8,530 feet, were shrouded by a pewter sky and driving drizzle. Undaunted, Kaplinski knew that patience would be rewarded. First one, then another, would cast off its mantle of gray, allowing a spotlight of sun to enshrine their snow-capped peaks. Working fast, he used a saturated red sable brush on dry paper to outline with clarity the first peak as the sun exposed it, then onto the next, as the scene rapidly changed in front of him. Then they were gone. Raindrops began to add some unwanted elements to his composition.

Kaplinski boarded a boat that would transport him from the base of the Cordillera del Paine across Lake Pehoe to his hostel, Refugio Pehoe, a couple of miles away. His companions aboard, mostly climbers who had tested their mettle on the Torres, mumbled assurances to this strangely outfitted American carrying a drawing pad and a clumsy box, that the weather should clear tomorrow. The gray clouds above and steel-hued chop on Lake Pehoe did not look promising.

Kaplinski painting Torres del Paine, Chile, 2003.

The next few days brought more of the same, yet in every mood and weather these awesome peaks defied anecdotal depiction and needed no figures as surrogates to pull the viewer into these intimidating scenes. While viewing the Cuernos del Paine from the vantage point of Lake Pehoe, Kaplinski had a brief moment when the clouds broke up and a wide swath of sunlight shone on the twin horns that crown the mountaintops. His brushes flew. He had only moments before the scudding clouds, fleet as shadow boxers, would engulf the peaks. He created a watercolor of cool blue-gray peaks contrasted with a turbulent gray-white sky that suggests all of the vastness and terrifying power of these sentinels in the Andes.

The final leg of this journey took Kaplinski north of the Strait of Magellan into Argentina's Los Glaciares National Park. The park contains about half of the 5,400-square-mile Patagonian Ice Field, an area roughly the size of Connecticut, and the largest ice mantle outside Antarctica. Of the park's forty-seven large glaciers, the two largest, Glaciar Upsala and Glaciar Viedma off of Lago Viedma, cover over 220 square miles each. Some 200 smaller glaciers, independent from the main

The Cuernos from Lake Pehoe, watercolor, 17" x 25" 2003. Collection of John and Lynn Fritschel.

ice field, seem insignificant in comparison, measuring less than one square mile each. Kaplinski's goal lay not at the end of Lago Viedma, but at the end of the one-hundred-mile-long Lago Argentino. Rounding the Península Magallenes, he came to the base of the 20-mile-wide Glaciar Perito Moreno. Due to its cyclical recession and advancement, and its regular launching of spectacular igloo icebergs, this impressive monster is the park's most famous glacier.

Observation points at various levels afforded views of the encroaching glacier. Drizzle and wind-whipped conditions persisted. Kaplinski huddled over his watercolor pad somehow finding the means to capture the crisp blue and white hues of the glacier while fighting the fluidity caused by errant raindrops. As Kaplinski began his descent from the middle balcony of the glacier overlook, gigantic 150-foot-high ice columns calved off from the body of the glacier and toppled into the icy water below—a chilling reminder of the titanic energy surrounding him.

That evening, comfortably settled in El Calafate 49 miles from the park, bruised by his paint box which the intemperate Patagonian wind had smashed against his leg, Kaplinski entertained a fleeting doubt. He wondered if he'd

El Grande Tempano – Big Iceberg, **acrylic on canvas, 30" x 40" 2003.**

gone too far, perhaps even over the edge, in search of inspiration. However enticing its majesty, this stark and windswept region had failed to attract other artists. French Impressionists had originally limited their outings to the comfort of Argenteuil, a short distance from Paris, to paint canoeists on the smooth waters of the Seine, navigated by gaily clad delicate women seated in their bows under colorful umbrellas to shield them from the sun. How dull, he thought, how bland . . . how convenient!

The next morning, although his drawing pad was constantly under threat of being blown to the far reaches of Patagonia, Kaplinski surrendered again to the drama of the ice fields before him. Prior to this trip, the artist had studied glaciology to better understand the nature of ice. He had a comrade-in-interest in nineteenth-century American painter, Frederic Church. Like Kaplinski, he painted with audacity. Church also had an "unquenchable ardor for travel" and had studied the nature of glaciation before embarking on a month-long trip to study Arctic icebergs and iceflows.

Exploration of vast, yet-to-be-charted polar regions captivated nineteenth-century audiences in much the same way as space probes attracts the interest of the American public today. In June 1859, Church hired a schooner to take him close to the ice floes off of Newfoundland. An excerpt from the voyage's chronicler, Louis Legrand Noble, imparts the exhilaration the party felt upon sighting their Arctic quarry: "'Icebergs! Icebergs!'—The cry brought us upon deck at sunrise. There they were, two of them, a large one and a smaller; the latter pitched upon the dark and misty desert of the sea like an Arab's tent; and the larger like a domed mosque in marble of a greenish white . . . enthroned on the deep in lonely majesty, the dread of mariners, and the wonder of the traveller, it was one of those imperial creations of nature that awaken powerful emotions, and illumine the imagination." [3]

The hardships and threats from the elements that Kaplinski suffered in painting glaciers in Alaska and Patagonia, also plagued Church on his Arctic journey. Besides running the danger of an iceberg destroying the boat, Church suffered from seasickness as he struggled to paint against a heavy sea, lashing his canvases to the mast of the heaving ship. His perilous journey ended successfully—memorialized in his 1863 oil painting, *Icebergs*.

In describing icebergs, Church wrote about their color and immensity, describing them as "a vast metropolis in ice, pearly white and red as roses, glittering in the sunset." [4] In his preliminary sketch notes, he also wrote about the iceberg's "exquisite opalescent blue-green." [5] Kaplinski also remarked on the coloration, a "unique, marvelous manganese blue." Although Ferdinand Magellan's explanation for the distinctive blue was simply extreme age of the formations, Kaplinski had the advantage of reading studies done by glaciologists. One writer has offered this more scientific analysis of the glacial blue:

> [T]he bluish cast was determined by the distinctive properties of snow and ice. The surface of snow and ice reflects all light, without preference for any particular color of the spectrum, but the interior handles light differently. Snow acts as a light filter, and treats the spectrum preferentially, scattering red light more strongly than blue. Photons emerging from snow and ice generally have more blue rays than red. The deeper the snow and ice, the farther the light must travel, and the darker blue it becomes, just as water appears a deeper blue as it increased in depth. For this reason, the deep crevasses in the glaciers possess an unearthly azure hue. [6]

Never an entire study of blues and whites, Kaplinski's glacial scenes anchor the ever-moving, groaning, ice fields to the walls of the peaks from which, over centuries, they have marched slowly to their destruction, piece by piece, in the valleys below.

Kaplinski left the lyricism of the Andes and headed back to Denver. Studio works to be developed from some of his on-the-spot scenes of Patagonia would have to wait. A commission from the City of Denver had languished too long on his desk, and as he settled back in his seat with the shoestring coastline of Chile far below him, images of Colorado's red rocks began to slowly displace those of the rugged mountains and sparkling glaciers of Patagonia.

Frederic Church, *Icebergs,* oil on canvas, 11 ½" x 18 ½" 1863. Collection of Mattatuck Museum, Waterbury, Connecticut.

CHAPTER 15

RED ROCKS, COLORADO: FROM THE BEAT OF THE TOM-TOM TO THE CLAMOUR OF THE GRATEFUL DEAD

Red Rocks Park, Colorado. **Drawing by Buffalo Kaplinski.**

As architect Burnham Hoyt drove from his office in downtown Denver toward the foothills west of the city, he caught the first glimpse of his objective. It rose dramatically out of the Dakota Hogback, a sharply crested ridge of shale and sandstone stretching along the Front Range of the Colorado Rockies. Just outside the small town of Morrison, three-hundred-foot-high monoliths of red-layered sandstone formed a natural amphitheater. Hoyt envisioned past performers on the nature's stage set between rock formations—ceremonial dances of the Ute and Arapaho driven by the beat of the drum; and the plaintive strains of "Ave Maria" sung by Mary Gardner, the world-famous Scottish soprano of the early 1900s, who arrived by horseback to perform one of the first concerts in this natural arena. She commented on the perfect acoustics. After climbing to the top of the amphitheater, she could hear the nuances of each note played by her accompanist one hundred and fifty feet below.

Hoyt's architectural assignment was a difficult one. George Cranmer, Denver's Manager of Parks and Improvements, envisioned in this remarkable park, purchased by the City of Denver in 1928, a world-class outdoor amphitheater challenging those found in Greece and Sicily. How then, to design seating, orchestra pit, dressing rooms, access, and related facilities, while preserving the original flavor of this majestic natural setting?

Historians suggest that Hoyt followed the pattern of the theater dedicated to Dionysus (the God of wine in Greek mythology) in Athens.[1] His genius, however, was understatement. When it came to architectural design, he believed in simplicity. At Red Rocks he entered into a collaboration with nature. The great monoliths on each side of the stage suffered only the addition of tastefully designed stone towers for dressing rooms and equipment. And the red rock formation at the base of the amphitheater provided a textured backdrop for the red concrete proscenium. For landscaping Hoyt used local juniper trees, placed in native red sandstone planter boxes which, tidily, but without noticeable formality, separate the interior sandstone seating from the stairs on the perimeter of the theater. The complex, completed in 1941, looked "as if it had grown on the spot, emerging from the earth as the stones around it had."[2] Performers, patrons, and architects have since praised it. The amphitheater was selected as the most notable twentieth-century structure for the American Institute of Architects 1956 Centennial exhibit at the National Academy of Art in Washington, D.C. From its modern inception the amphitheater has hosted pop to classical and comedian to dramatic performances with the distant lights of downtown Denver as a backdrop.

Hoyt had envisioned one further improvement which was not incorporated in his original construction drawings. As one exits a tunnel through an outcropping of red rocks north of the amphitheater and progresses up to the west rim of the amphitheater, a visitors' center complete with conference center, restaurant, and performers' hall of fame, has been blended into the upper base of the amphitheater. In the early design phase of the visitors center Hoyt's conservative concept was threatened by opportunistic commercialism. This was reined in by Friends of Red Rocks, a community-based organization dedicated to the preservation of the natural landscape and Hoyt's compatible design. The Center was completed in 2003 and only implementation of Denver's Public Art Program remained.

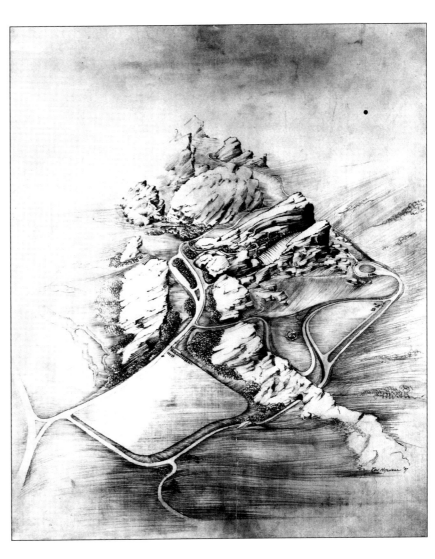

Red Rocks Amphitheater conceptual drawing for Burnham Hoyt's design, 1937. Denver Public Library Western History Collection.

Like other communities across the country, Denver Public Arts had budgeted one percent of the construction cost for artistic enhancement. And so a call to artists was made. One hundred and eighty-two artists from all over the United States responded with resumes and slides of their work. In early 2003 a public art evaluation panel selected eight entries from among these applicants' submissions. Steve Good, a member of the panel and respected art historian, recalled how Kaplinski's slides, presented anonymously with the others, stood out. His style, palette, and sensitivity to the landscape "made him a natural for this project." As with the Johns-Manville commission, the panel permitted Kaplinski and the other participating artists great latitude in the interpretation of Red Rocks Park. [3]

Kaplinski went to work immediately, traversing the appointed landscape first through a blanket of snow laid by a late winter storm. He began creating a series of plein-air paintings which captured the solitude of the place—broken only by a hawk and his mate making wide circles above the towering monuments. The majesty of these eroded sentinels was enhanced by the contrasting snow on which they cast, in the eyes of the artist, elongated shadows of varying shades of blue.

As springtime approached, the snow melted and was absorbed into the scree in which junipers and aspen trees fight for survival. Kaplinski waited for the pale green leaves of the aspen to sprout. Retracing his steps from his earlier treks in the snow, he now found softer light. The red sandstone outcroppings provided an elegant gateway to the distant blue-green vegetation beyond. As the seasons wore on, Kaplinski became engrossed in the nuances of his favorite sites, dressed differently for each of his visits, according to the season. Each of his plein-air interpretations of the park offers a distinctive mood, yet, as with Antonio Vivaldi's musical interpretation of the four seasons in his violin concertos, a singular interpretation of one season piques an expectation of what the other seasons offer. Although Kaplinski made many sketches through the seasons, he had to choose and interpret one.

Few are likely to question the merit of the fall study he chose to expand to a four-by-five-foot acrylic on canvas. This painting, entitled *A Masterpiece in Stone,* now hangs above the hearth in the Red Rocks Visitor Center. It invites one to shut out, for a moment, the din of activity in the room and listen

A Masterpiece In Stone, acrylic on canvas, 48" x 60" 2003. Collection of The City and County of Denver.

for the Ute drummers and their mournful song drifting among the magnificent red rocks Kaplinski has brought inside—leaving the interpretation up to the viewer, fresh from wandering among them.

The dedication of Kaplinski's work and that of the other commissioned artists was held on a snowy, wind-swept evening in December 2003 at the Visitor Center, reminding those who braved it, that stormy weather in the Rocky Mountains is always a force to be reckoned with. However, the warm hues of Kaplinski's red rocks enriched by the mellow tones of the crackling fire in the hearth, over which his painting presides, provided a cheerful welcome and assurance of unhurried enjoyment of the evening and the artists' works.

Denver's newly-elected mayor John Hickenlooper's remarks to collectors and friends of the artists, representatives of Denver's Office of Art, Culture

Dedication of Visitor Center at Red Rocks Park, Colorado 2003. Buffalo and Vicky Kaplinski with Honorable John Hickenlooper, Mayor of Denver, Colorado.

and Film, members of Friends of Red Rocks, and some old-timers who had worked in the construction of the amphitheater more than sixty years earlier, declared him a friend of the arts. "Nature as reflected in these magnificent red rocks made the call," he observed, "and these talented artists responded."

In its short history, Burnham Hoyt's legacy to the people of Denver has been threatened, protected, and now artistically fulfilled. The sounds of music redounding from its red rock walls live on, ever-changing, from the pedantic beat of the tom-tom, through symphonic tones wrought under the baton of Leonard Bernstein, to the clamour of the Grateful Dead. The visual and performing arts are at home among the monoliths of time.

When Johns-Manville awarded Kaplinski a commission to document the landscapes of Ken Caryl Ranch, his stars were just beginning to rise. This vote of confidence meant much to the young artist at that point in his career. Thirty years later the Red Rocks commission brought Kaplinski long-deserved public approbation as an established artist. In the eyes of the City of Denver and citizens of Colorado he had not only arrived, he had become one of the state's singular artists.

SHOWTIME AT THE KAPLINSKI RANCH

By 1983 many of the galleries that had represented Kaplinski no longer existed. Many of the dealers that he respected had gone out of business. Sandra Wilson sold her gallery in 1980; Wally Baehler and Jim Fisher closed their doors within a few years. Known for weathering boom-or-bust cycles, a slump in the oil industry and the economy of Denver, coupled with a recession, had a great effect on the city's art market. The outspoken Kaplinski had another gripe. In 1983 the *Rocky Mountain News* quoted him as saying: "My feeling is that today's art galleries are filled with junk and second-rate art. I don't think they are doing the job they should be doing for the artist or for the collector. . . . They keep asking higher and higher percentages—with nothing in return."[1] Kaplinski lamented the loss of the active, exciting art scene that he'd experienced five years earlier. At that juncture, with some exceptions, Kaplinski began to rent vacant spaces in lower downtown Denver to exhibit and promote his own work. Some years earlier he had begun hosting studio shows at his ranch in Elizabeth for his patrons and friends.

Behemoth of Dallas Divide, **acrylic on canvas, 34" x 60" 1968. Collection of Mr. and Mrs. Jim Lamson.**

Maroon Bells, Aspen, **plein-air watercolor, 14" x 32" 1996. Collection of Mr. and Mrs. Rick Jergenson.**

Galleries showing Kaplinski's work have generally succumbed to his rantings that sales out of his studio enhance exposure and interest in his work. For the collector, a visit to the studio is a happening. The end of the trail is a dusty road wandering southwest from the Town of Elizabeth—a one-hour drive from Denver—and there is no mistaking the stylized orange buffalo hanging from a pine post directing the visitor to his studio. Once inside, there's no shortage of banter. A lot of stored-up energy is released; and stories, lies, a bone-crushing handshake or hug greet the visitor entering the barn-converted-to-studio adorned with Kaplinski's current splashes of color.

Kaplinski's studio shows began in 1975. These early affairs were modest: tequila and popcorn served up after Kaplinski demonstrated his political leanings by introducing other members of the ranch family, pet pigs Pat, Dick, and Spiro—actually likely to snort in response to any admiration.

More recently these events treat the visitor to a well-organized exhibition, professionally lit and hung, of his current work with a few pieces from past decades to provide some perspective on his artistic growth and career. In the course of the July, 2003 show of works from his trip to Patagonia, Kaplinski moved through the studio—talking, explaining, joking. In thanking a purchaser of several of his paintings, he exclaimed, "Now Vicky will be able to put food on the table for another week, and purchase other essentials like toothpaste and deodorant—" A voice from a far corner of the studio broke in, "We'll all be grateful for that!" Later on, noting lines of pink and yellow extending down the side of an aspen tree depicted in an otherwise subdued forest study, a collector remarked, "How in the world did you come up with those colors?" Kaplinski retorted, "If you smoked what I had smoked, you'd see it too!"

This discussion inevitably led to one of his favorite subjects: the Purkinje shift. Kaplinski is serious about his color, and all kidding aside, is quick to point out that a blaze of color is not an end in itself. In his paintings it is a true image—the very thing that drew him to the subject. The color shift comes with a change in illumination: in high illumination the reds, yellows and oranges are brightest; in dim illumination greens and blues dominate. The same foliage at high noon on sunlit day will sparkle with reds, yellows, oranges, and

Aspen Elegance, acrylic on canvas, 30" x 40" 1985.

white reflected light yet will radiate greens and blues at twilight. For emphasis Kaplinski will add a pink or violet to primary colors. Armed with that explanation the collector might first be moved to ask, "At what time of day was this painted?" The answer to that question brings us closer to understanding Kaplinski's color selection.

Retracing the route to the Kaplinski studio and heading home after one of these studio shows, typically held in the early evening, a guest's color sense and perception of the landscape stay turned on high. Headlights from a lone vehicle proceeding down a gentle hill in the distance, barely adding to the reflected golden light on the grassy fields, is an instant reminder of Peter Hurd's ability to capture such conflicting light and mood. Yet, it is difficult to resist noting where Kaplinski might add some violet to selected shadows. Or the last glow of the orange sun silhouetting the horizontal cap of Long's Peak may provoke an image of Dan Namingha's beloved Hekytwi Mesa in Arizona at sunset. In Kaplinski's interpretation of the same scene, the viewer has come to expect him to add a splash of purple or pink for emphasis. Like the reversal of color sense in the Purkinje shift, Kaplinski sharpens one's ability to perceive and understand, compare and contrast, sometimes gently, other times forcefully, but never without effect. With this accomplishment Kaplinski exceeded even his own expectations. His work had grown beyond what he told the judge in Georgetown that his paintings would do on the historic day of his name change some thirty years earlier.

EPILOGUE: SUNSETS, GRAPES, AND FINE WINE

Looking back over the past forty years of Buffalo Kaplinski's artistic life, many aspects of his career have come full circle. Some aspects have been repeated in a renewed form. Once a student with some memorable mentor-teachers, he has carried on the teacher-mentor legacy he inherited in Chicago. Shortly after he moved to Denver, he taught at the Colorado Institute of Art. Later he served as a faculty member of the Art Students League of Denver (1987-1989) in its early years. Over the past few decades he has taught numerous workshops.

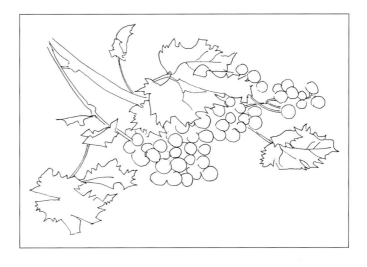

Grapes Ripening on the Western Slope, Colorado. **Drawing by Buffalo Kaplinski.**

In the mid-1990s, Kaplinski revisited another aspect connected with his Chicago years. Drawing upon his earlier skills as an illustrator, without the restraints usually imposed by product advertising, Kaplinski accepted a commission from Plum Creek Cellars to create labels for the company's wines. Reducing the splendor of the Grand Canyon, sixteen miles across and one mile deep, with all its rapidly changing nuances of color, to a small two-dimensional surface was challenge enough. Colorado's wine country, the epicenter of which is commonly ascribed to the Grand Valley area around Grand Junction, posed a similar challenge to Kaplinski—only this time in miniature.

The labels he created hold their own as artistic works. Many are miniature watercolors, quickly grasped, yet provide pleasant impressions. Kaplinski recognized the beauty in the rows of grape-laden vines, suggesting paths to the mountains beyond. Perhaps Van Gogh found similar comfort in the rows of olive trees at Saint-Rémy.

Indulging in a brief analysis of the merchandizing, there is no mistaking that these diminutive scenes accomplish their objective: the redstone invites the consumer to anticipate a rich full-bodied Cabernet, the brilliant red and yellow leaves on mountain ash and aspen trees suggest a buttery Chardonnay, and the blues and whites of a snowy mountain scene conjure up the image of a smooth, cool Riesling.

The Observation Point – Phantom Canyon, Colorado, **plein-air acrylic on canvas, 36" x 24" 2004. Collection of Mr. and Mrs. Rick Jergenson.**

Kaplinski's posters for the annual September Winefest in the Grand Valley were one of several drawing cards to this once sleepy area on Colorado's Western Slope. Sounds of music, the clink of wine glasses, and murmurs of wine tasters are appropriate accompaniment to shadows cast by surrounding mountains and mesas stretching lazily across the valley floor in the late afternoon. But how can these commercial concerns be reconciled with a landscape artist who has searched around the world for landscapes that extol the drama of nature or the eloquence and harmony of nature and man? There will, of course, be achievements in the development of the wine industry like any other. More land will be altered, and perhaps the area will become more populous. These are the concerns of every landscape painter.

When writing about Kaplinski's achievements as a landscape artist in the early 1970s, the words of John Jellico seem just as appropriate now as then. Jellico remarked on the unusual artist who had the power to convey a vivid sense of his own feelings in his paintings. "His landscapes convey the beauty and vitality of simple objects, and he expresses his responses by the daring use of design and color in new and surprising color harmonies and by the vigor of his brush strokes. His passion imbues his landscape paintings with a tumultuous motion. In all of his work there is an amazing range of qualities; throughout, a remarkable luminosity prevails." [1]

Redstone, **watercolor, courtesy of Plum Creek Cellars, Palisade, Colorado.**

Recognition of Kaplinski's achievements has also reunited him with the group of Taos, then Denver, artists who shared hard beginnings. In the last decade, several art institutions have featured him and his fellow "Denver School" artists in group shows. In 1992 the National Cowboy Hall of Fame in Oklahoma City held a retrospective show for many of them billed as *Seven From Denver.* The "Seven" included Ken Bunn, George Carlson, Len Chmiel, Mark Daily, Buffalo Kaplinski, Bill Sharer and Jon Zahourek.

The exhibition of these artists' work not only showed how they had matured in their approach to art—but also the specific times and places where

Chardonnay, **watercolor, courtesy of Plum Creek Cellars, Palisade, Colorado.**

Reisling, **watercolor, courtesy of Plum Creek Cellars, Palisade, Colorado.**

they had painted and sculpted. Looking back to those experiences in Taos and Denver, Kaplinski remembered: "It was the respect for each other's work that bound us together, and because of that respect we were willing to share what we did—landscapes, galleries and patrons."

In 1998 the Foothills Art Gallery in Golden, Colorado, honored the centennial of the Taos art colony's founding with two exhibitions. The second one, *100 Years of the Art of Taos*, for the first time established links between the Taos founders and the "Denver School" of painters and sculptors. Among them were Kaplinski, Ned Jacob, Bill Sharer, and George Carlson, who had

At National Cowboy Hall of Fame, 1992. *Left to right*: **Jon Zahourek, George Carlson, Buffalo Kaplinski, and Len Chmiel.**

formed an "emigré mini-colony" in Taos in the 1960s. Reviewing that show, *Denver Post* critic remarked: "The psychedelic pink "Casa Rosa" of Buffalo Kaplinski from Elizabeth is offset by Dali trees and blue snow, while lurid acrylics turn his "Eternal Canyon" into an abstract vision." [2]

Perhaps the greatest recognition comes from Kaplinski's collectors. Remarking about one collector who recently purchased a painting, Kaplinski said: "He has thirty of my paintings, he doesn't need another one. Yet he loved this painting so much that he had to buy it. I got the nicest note from him. It said: 'As always, your art enriches our lives, and we are very grateful for that.' And I thought, wow, now that is really cool. To have that kind of statement when they've got a virtual museum of my work in their home."

Silence, **acrylic on canvas, 40" x 30" 1985. Collection of Roger B. Smith.**

Asked where he would like to travel next, Kaplinski responds "Africa." While he longs to lay eyes on the adobe cities of Timbuktu and Djenné in Mali, along with some other places in Africa, the health and political risks there have made him consider other options. As dreams of seeing Africa fade, he remembers his vow to return to Alaska's ice fields, to the glaciers' manganese

Kaplinski at his Ranch in Elizabeth, Colorado 1985.

blue. That color still haunts him; his eye has not yet had enough. The true epilogue of this book remains unwritten. It surely will include more glacial rumblings and hues.

Through his adventures in the American West and in the far reaches of the world, Kaplinski has demonstrated that there is no shortage of scenes, color, and light—the ingredients which have inspired changes in his composition, palette, and technique. Kaplinski has challenged the narrow sense of place adopted by many competent and respected artists before him. What lies beyond familiar scenes near home not only challenges the artist—expanding his ability to interpret—but also, for a moment, takes the viewer to a familiar place or to one where he would like to be.

NOTES

Chapter 1

1. Alan Gussow, *A Sense of Place: The Artist and the American Landscape*, 27.
2. Ibid., 27, 30.
3. Jean Bouret, *The Barbizon School*, New York Graphic Society Ltd., 1973, p. 29.
4. Dore Ashton, *Picasso on Art: A Selection of Views*, Da Capo Press, Inc., 1972, p. 127.
5. Drawn in part from John Jellico, "The Infinite Landscapes of Buffalo Kaplinski," *American Artist*, August 1972: 24.
6. From an interview quoted in Frances Traher, "Buffalo Kaplinski Side-stepping the Expected; Moving On," *Art West*, Sept. 1984.
7. Claude Monet's *The Road to Vitheuil*, 1879, exemplifies his quest to "paint light itself." The elongated blue shadows from the trees lining the road add brilliance and contrast to this sun-drenched painting.

Chapter 2

1. Source: BK: Selected Bio Info ca. 1998-99.
2. Francis Traher, *Art West*, September/October 1984, p. 47.
3. Ibid., Kaplinski biographical sketch 9 February 1999.
4. Information from Buffalo Kaplinski, and Traher, *Art West*, Sept/Oct 1984: 47-48
5. Interviews with George Carlson, 31 October 2003; 10 November 2003.
6. This discussion of Kaplinski's technique is based on text written by Sally Schrup, artist, writer and editor in Taos, New Mexico. The author gratefully acknowledges her insight into his mode of working.
7. Traher, *Art West*, Sept/Oct 1984: 48; *Denver Post*, 30 August 1970.

Chapter 3

1. Laura Bickerstaff, *Pioneer Artists of Taos*, Old West Publishing Co., 1955, p. 13.
2. Rosie Stewart MS, p. 9.
3. Sandra Dallas, *Sacred Paint – Ned Jacob*, Fenn Galleries Publishing, Inc., 1979, p. 65.
4. Stewart MS, p. 5.
5. Interview with George Carlson, 10 November 2003; interview with Ned Jacob, 23 November 2004.
6. Interview with George Carlson, 10 November 2003.
7. Interview with Ned Jacob, 11 November 2003.
8. Interview with Jon Zahourek, 19 November 2003.
9. The Denver-Taos Circle of Artists included at various times George Carlson, Mark Daily, Ned Jacob, Buffalo Kaplinski, William E. Sharer, Jon Zahourek, Antonio Mendoza, Hank Folwell, and Eugene Dobos. Sandra Dallas, *Sacred Paint – Ned Jacob*,

Fenn Galleries Publishing Inc., 1979, Photo p. 60.

10. "The Hard Bright Light of the West" Rick Romancito, Tempo, *Taos News,* 22 May 1997, C12.

11. Interview with William E. Sharer, 4 November 2003.

12. Interview with George Carlson, 10 November 2003.

13. Marlan Miller, "Galleries in Santa Fe, Taos Display Real Vigor," *Phoenix Gazette,* 30 August 1966.

14. Don Blair, "Buffalo Kaplinski," Blair Galleries, Ltd. brochure, 13-27 August 1967.

Chapter 4

1. "Western Talent," Denver, Colorado: Rive Gauche Gallery, October [ ] 1967.

2. Owen Gallery text, 7-29 March 1969.

3. Cézanne "used carefully modulated color to enhance the formal qualities of his work, and developed a type of brushwork that increased the structural emphasis he sought." A Guide to Civilization, Kenneth Clark, p. 108.

4. *Denver Post,* 30 August 1970.

5. Interview with Jon Zahourek, 19 November 2003.

Chapter 5

1. Reference here made to Pierre Bonnard's painting, *The Terrace,* 1918.

2. "Buffalo Kaplinski: A Watercolor Documentary of Central America," ca. 1968-1971.

3. Bernal Días del Castillo, soldier in Hernán Cortés' army, recalling the Spaniards' first view of Tenochtitlan, capital of the Aztec empire in November 1519, in *America's Ancient Cities* by Fene S. Stuart, Washington D.C.: National Geographic Society, 1988. p, 9.

4. *Recent works by Buffalo Kaplinski,* Denver, Colorado: Owen Gallery, 26 March-15 April 1971

5. *Denver Post,* 30 August 1970.

6. The other artists selected were painters Ed Jagman, Charles Jacoby, Jeannie Pear and Hal Shelton; sculptor Ken Bunn, and photographers Robert Koropp, James Milmoe, and Dick Spas. For further information on this project and the history of Ken Caryl Ranch, see "A Heritage: The Manville Corporation Ken-Caryl Art Collection."

7. Rosie Stewart MS, p. 2.

Chapter 6

1. Diane Ray, "The Greeley Art Scene" *Greeley Tribune,* 29 September 1976: 33.

2. Other members of the core group Wilson represented in Denver were painters Mark Daily, Len Chmiel and sculptor Kenneth Bunn.

3. Interview with William Sharer, 4 November 2003.

4. Interview with Len Chmiel, 5 November 2003.

5. Interview with Sandra Wilson, 15 March 2004.

6. Interview with George Carlson, 17 June 2004.

7. Interview with Jerry Ravenscroft, Spring, 2003.

Chapter 7

1. Kaplinski made this trip in August 1980 with his friend, Al Vatter, a microcell biologist and collector of Native American art, who shared Kaplinski's sense of adventure. Later Vatter and his wife, Marilyn, began collecting Kaplinski's work and had a show of his paintings at their Deer Dancer gallery.

Chapter 8

1. Interview with George Carlson, 14 April 2004.

2. Powell, *Exploration of the Colorado River* p. 174 in Joni Louise Kinsey, *Thomas Moran and the Surveying of the American West*, p. 108.

3. Thomas Moran to Mary Nimmo Moran, August 13, 1873, in Kinsey, p. 105.

4. Interview with Len Chmiel, 5 November 2003.

5. Bill Richards, "The Untamed Yellowstone," *National Geographic,* August 1981, page 257.

6. See Alan Gussow, *A Sense of Place, The Artist and the American Land.* Friends of the Earth, Inc., 1971. p. 77.

7. Kinsey, *Thomas Moran and the Surveying of the American West,* p.65.

8. James Mills, "New Kaplinski Works Show His Exhilaration," *Denver Post,* November 4, 1979.

9. Betty Harvey, *Artists of the Rockies* September 1977.

10. David Boyer, "Yosemite – Forever", *National Geographic,* January 1985, p. 53.

11. *Yosemite and Beyond: Paintings by Buffalo Kaplinski.* Reno, Nevada: Stremmel Galleries, 7-21 June 1980.

12. Marjorie Barrett, *Rocky Mountain News* "Now" Sunday 9 April 1978: 3.

Chapter 9

1. Vincent Scully, *The Earth, The Temple, and the Gods*, Yale University Press, 1962, p. 157.

2. "Artist widens subject horizons," *Rocky Mountain News*, [ca. 13 October] 1983.

3. Max Price, "Artist's Horizon Broadened," *Denver Post,* 13 October 1983.

Chapter 10

1. Traher, *Art West* 1984, p. 44.
2. Max Price, "Kaplinski Turns to Painting of Ancient Cultures," *Denver Post*, 16 November 1984: 31.

Chapter 11

1. A detailed account of Bligh's Fiji adventure may be found in Leonard Wibberley, *Fiji: Islands of the Dawn*, Ives Washburn, Inc., N.Y., 1964, and of his perilous escape to Timor in Sam McKinney, *Bligh*, International Marine Pub. Co., 1989.

2. Gauguin's life in Tahiti and his secluded tropical studio are well documented in Bengt Banielsson, *Gauguin In the South Seas*, Doubleday & Co., Inc., 1966.

Chapter 12

1. Rosie Stewart MS, p.20.
2. Stewart MS, p.18.
3. Ibid.
4. Interview with Vicky Kaplinski, 27 April 2004.

Chapter 13

1. *Literary Chronicle and Weekly Review*, January 4, 1823, p. 15.
2. *Spectator*, June 8, 1833, p. 529.

Chapter 14

1. Ian Cameron, *Magellan And The First Circumnavigation of the World*, Saturday Review Press, N.Y., 1973, p. 48.
2. The San Antonio, captained by Magellan's cousin, suffered mutiny halfway through the strait and the deserters sailed the ship directly back to Spain. Only three of Magellan's original command of five ships made it through the strait to the Pacific. Tim Joyner, *Magellan*, International Marine, 1942, p. 158.
3. Louis Legrand Noble, *After Icebergs with a Painter: A Summer Voyage to Labrador and Around Newfoundland*. New York: Appleton and Company; London: Sampson Low and Son, 1861: 108 in Eleonore Harvey. *The Voyage of the Icebergs: Frederic Church's Arctic Masterpiece*. Dallas Museum of Art, 2002: 90
4. Information on F. E. Church from Mattatuck Museum, Mattatuck Historical Society website, description of its Church painting, *Icebergs*, 1863.
5. Harvey, *The Voyage of the Icebergs*, 47.

6. Lawrence Bergreen, *Over The Edge Of The World*, Harper Collins Publishers, Inc., 2003, p. 180.

Chapter 15

1. Mary Voelz Chandler, *Guide to Denver Architecture*, Westcliffe Publishers, 2001, p. 345.
2. Ibid.
3. Other artists commissioned by the City of Denver for the Red Rocks Visitor Center Public Art Project, 2003 included Stephen Batura, Jim Colbert, Joellyn Duesberry, Carole Fitzgerald, William Stockman, Judith Thomlinson Trager, and Christy Wyckoff.

Chapter 16

1. Marjorie Barrett, "Disgruntled artist severs gallery ties," *Rocky Mountain News*, 13 January 1983: 83.

Epilogue: Sunsets, Grapes, and Fine Wine

1. John Jellico, "The Infinite Landscapes of Buffalo Kaplinski," *American Artist*, August 1972: 24.
2. Jeff Bradley, "Foothills Exhibition Traces 100 years of Taos Artistry," *Denver Post*, 31 January 1999.

BUFFALO KAPLINSKI EXHIBITIONS

1965:
140th Annual Exhibition. New York, New York: American Watercolor Society.
98th Annual Exhibition. New York, New York: National Academy of Art.
Exhibition: Illinois State Fair. Award: Honorable Mention.
One-Man Show, Milwaukee, Wisconsin: L'Atelier Galleries.

1966:
Resident Artists, Taos, New Mexico: Stables Gallery.
One-Man Show. Milwaukee, Wisconsin: L'Atelier Galleries.
Ashe Emmett Exhibit: Chicago, Illinois.
Taos Group Show. Colorado Springs, Colorado: Colorado Springs Fine Arts Center.

1967:
One-Man Show. Milwaukee, Wisconsin: L'Atelier Galleries.
Western Talent. Denver, Colorado: Rive Gauche Gallery.
Western Talent. Darien, Connecticut: Rive Gauche Gallery.
The Changing Image of the Indian. Santa Fe, New Mexico: Museum of Fine Arts, 16 April-
    18 June 1967. *The Prophets of Oraibi,* no. 70, wc. Works by Buffalo Kaplinski, Ned
    Jacob, Bill Sharer, Fritz White and Jon Zahourek, loaned by Blair Galleries, Ltd.
Own Your Own Show. Denver, Colorado: Denver Art Museum.
Junior League Show. Oklahoma City, Oklahoma.
Buffalo Kaplinski. Santa Fe, New Mexico: Blair Gallery, 13-27 August 1967. *Sky of the
    Kachinas,* no. 1; *As Each Fledgling Leaves,* no. 2; *Ramble, Wander – My Way,* no. 3; *Stone
    Catapult,* no. 4; *Kw A Toko, The Upper Air,* no. 5; *Only My Eyes,* no. 6; *Night Pueblo,*
    no. 7; *Sky Make Talk,* no. 8; *Autumn Hunter,* no. 9; *Exploring the Canyon,* no. 10; *Ruin
    Patterns,* no. 11; *Canyon Depths,* no. 2; *Two Sages in the Wind,* no. 13; *Prophets of Oraibi,*
    no. 14; *Mission Church,* no. 15; *The Idler,* no. 16; *Pueblo Sunlight,* no. 17, *Spider Woman
    Legend Thoughts,* no. 18.
Southwest Culture Exhibit. El Paso, Texas.
Western Artists. La Jolla, California: Jones Gallery.

1968:
One Man Show, Milwaukee, Wisconsin: L'Atelier Galleries.
One Man Show. Santa Fe, New Mexico: Blair Galleries.
One Man Watercolor Show. Denver, Colorado and Vail, Colorado: Rive Gauche Gallery.
Southwestern Artists: Five-man show. Denver, Colorado and Darien, Connecticut: Rive
    Gauche Gallery.
George Carlson and Buffalo Kaplinski. Denver, Colorado: Rive Gauche Gallery, May 1968.

Buffalo Kaplinski. Santa Fe, New Mexico: Blair Galleries. Brochure featured: *Mundo Verde, diptych 25" x 17"*.

Southwestern Artists: Four man show. Denver, Colorado: Museum of Natural History.

Southwestern Biennial Exhibition. Santa Fe, New Mexico: Museum of Fine Arts. Award: Honorable Mention.

Own Your Own Show. Denver, Colorado: Denver Art Museum.

Interim Show. Denver, Colorado: Denver Art Museum.

1969:

Recent Works by Buffalo Kaplinski, Ramon Kelley, Ned Jacob, Bill Sharer. Denver, Colorado: Owen Gallery, 7-29 March 1969. Brochure featured: *Call to the Moon*, wc 17" x 13" inches.

Own Your Own Show. Denver, Colorado: Denver Art Museum.

Kaplinski Retrospective Show. Denver, Colorado: Jewish Community Center.

23rd American Drawing Exhibition. Norfolk, Virginia: Norfolk Museum of Arts and Sciences.

Buffalo Kaplinski: Watercolorist of the Southwest. Denver, Colorado: Owen Gallery, 14 November – 4 December 1969.

Annual Open Show. Central City, Colorado: Gilpin County Galleries. Award: wc first place.

28th Exhibition: Painters and Sculptors Society of New Jersey. Jersey City, New Jersey.

Southwestern Watercolor Society Exhibition. Dallas, Texas: SMU Fine Arts Center. Purchase award. Traveling exhibition: Oklahoma City, Oklahoma: Oklahoma Art Center; San Antonio, Texas: Trinity University; Cheyenne, Wyoming: Cheyenne Art Guild; Austin, Texas: Laguna Gloria Art Museum.

One-Man Watercolor Show. Lindsborg, Kansas: Birger Sandzen Museum. Museum purchase for permanent collection.

Invitational One Man Show. Northfield, Minnesota: St. Olaf College.

Missouri Valley Drawing Competition. Topeka, Kansas: Washburn College.

Audubon Artists 27th Exhibition. New York, New York: National Arts Gallery.

162nd Annual Exhibition. Philadelphia, Pennsylvania: Pennsylvania Academy of the Fine Arts.

Southwestern Artists: Four Man Show. Denver, Colorado: Owen Gallery.

Denver United States Federal Center Exhibit. Denver, Colorado: United States Federal Center.

15th Exhibition National Society Painters. New York, New York. Award: casein honorable mention.

1971:

Recent works by Buffalo Kaplinski. Denver, Colorado: Owen Gallery. Brochure featured: *Lone Fisherman (Panama)*; *Harvest Houses (Guatamala).*

1975:

Chicago Tribune Bicentennial Art Collection. Chicago, Illinois: Jack O'Grady Galleries, Inc. Commissioned entry.

Buffalo Kaplinski Estes Park, Colorado: Gallery of the Ravens, 12-21 September 1975.

1976:

Len Chmiel-Buffalo Kaplinski. Denver, Colorado: Sandra Wilson Galleries. Brochure featured: *Sulfur Basin Fumes* (acrylic, 30" x 40"); *Winter Still Life—Blacktail Plateau* (wc 10" x 8").

1977:

The Colorado Exhibition. Arvada, Colorado: The Arvada Art Center, 26 March – 22 April 1977.

Catalogue featured: *Pikes Peak (From Elbert County Colo.).*

Twenty Westerns by America's Contemporaries. Chicago, Illinois: Jack O'Grady Galleries, Inc., 21 April – 26 May 1977. Catalogue featured: *Cumulus Clouds* (o/c 30" x 40"); *Rocky Mountain High* (o/c 30" x 40"); *Plains Showers* (acrylic 16" x 20").

1978:

Buffalo Kaplinski. Denver, Colorado: Sandra Wilson Galleries. Brochure featured: *High Country Cow Camp.*

1979:

Buffalo Kaplinski. Greeley, Colorado: Greeley National Bank, October 1979.

Buffalo Kaplinski: Recent Work. Denver, Colorado: Sandra Wilson Galleries.

1980:

Buffalo Kaplinski. Denver, Colorado: Carson Gallery of Western American Art. Brochure featured: *Tales from the Basket Makers.*

Yosemite and Beyond: Paintings by Buffalo Kaplinski. Reno, Nevada: Stremmel Galleries. Brochure featured: *Bridal Veil Falls-Yosemite* (acrylic wc 10 ½" x 13"); *Solar Drenched Canyon* (acrylic wc/board 12" x 17 ½"); *Cedaredge Mesas and Orchards* (on-the-spot ptg acrylic/bd 18" x 24").

1981:

Buffalo Kaplinski. Denver, Colorado: Carson Gallery of Western American Art. Catalogue included: *You're in Teton Country, Over by the Triangle*; *Owl Rock Totem Pole*; *His Creation/Our Delight*.

1983:

Kaplinski on Location in Greece. Denver, Colorado: The Deer Dancer. Brochure featured: *Byzantine Dome and Belltower/Santorini*; *Where the Colossus Stood/Rhodes*.

1984:

Exhibition. Denver, Colorado: Baehlers Fine Art Consulting. Brochure featured: *Crisp Afternoon, Grand Canyon* (Acrylic wc 10 ½" x 13 ½").

Ancient Lands of the Middle East by Buffalo Kaplinski. Denver, Colorado: James Fisher Gallery.

1985:

Buffalo Kaplinski. Denver, Colorado: James Fisher Gallery, 7-14 June 1985.

1986:

East Meets West. Denver, Colorado: Jewish Community Center, 14-24 May 1986.

1987:

Reflections in an Artist's Eye. Colorado Springs, Colorado: The Shops at Tiffany Square, 16-25 January 1987.

A Heritage: The Manville Corporation Ken-Caryl Art Collection. Denver, Colorado: Denver Chamber of Commerce. Catalogue included: *Giant Red Oxide Rock*, no. 28; *The Knowledge of the Sun*, no. 29; *On the Spot at Ken-Caryl Ranch*, nos. 38-44; *Space of the West*, no. 54; *On the Spot at Ken-Caryl Ranch*, nos. 127-129.

The Spell of Hawaii: Paintings by Buffalo Kaplinski. Mona Kea Hotel, Hawaii. Brochure featured: *Birds in Paradise*.

A Christmas Exhibition. Denver, Colorado: Saks Galleries. Works of master instructors: Doug Dawson, Madeline Wiener, Ramon Kelley, Bruce Cody, Buffalo Kaplinski, Veryl Goodnight, Mel Carter, Mark Thompson, Mark Daily, Dale Chisman, Emanuel Martinez, Kenneth Bunn, Kim English, Marti Lawrence.

1990:

Early Winter Studio Show: Paintings by Buffalo Kaplinski. Elizabeth, Colorado: Buffalo Kaplinski Studio, 20-21 January 1990.

Artists of America. Denver, Colorado: Colorado History Museum, 5 September – November 1990. Catalogue included: *Springtime Jigsaw Puzzle, Rocky Mountain National Park*.

1992:

From My Viewpoint: Watercolors and acrylics by Buffalo Kaplinski. Denver, Colorado: 1440 Blake Street, Denver, Colorado. Brochure featured: *A Winter's Sabbath Rest* (15" x 19" plein-air wc).

1993:

Seven from Denver. Oklahoma City, Oklahoma: National Cowboy Hall of Fame, 20 November – 17 March 1993. Catalogue included: *An Impressionist's Dream* (plein-air wc 14 ½" x 11"); *Canyon Lands Cubism* (wc 21" x 28"); *Goat House Ruins* (wc 12" x 29"); *Dolores River Overlook* (plein-air acrylic/canvas 20" x 24"); *The Master's Touch* (plein-air wc 16" x 20"); *Streams of Living Water, John 7:38* (plein-air wc 16" x 20"); *New Mantle of Snow, Telluride, Colorado* (plein-air wc 15 ¾" x 21 ¾"); *The Blue River, Silverthorne, Colorado* (plein-air wc 16" x 20"); *Oh Lord, How Excellent Are Your Works In All the Earth* (wc 29 ½" x 21 ¼"); *Gorge Over by Lizard Head Pass* (plein-air wc 22" x 14 ¾"). Retrospective works—not for sale: *Taos Window* 1970 (wc 9" x 12" coll. private); *Monument Valley* 1980 (wc 12" x 24" coll. Henry Meininger); *New Mexico Essay* 1975 (wc 16" x 26"); *Canyon Island Interpretation of the Grand Canyon* (acrylic 18" x 24" coll. M/M Malcolm G. Stewart); *Rio Grande Gorge in Ochre* 1975 (wc 24" x 30" coll. M/M Malcolm G. Stewart); *Resting Nomad* (wc 12" x 18" coll. Buffalo Kaplinski).

1994:

For the Beauty of the Earth: *Daniel Pinkham/Buffalo Kaplinski*. Estes Park, Colorado: Gallery of the Winds.

Colorado Governor's Invitational Show. Loveland, Colorado: Loveland Museum.

Spanish Treasures, Moroccan Mosaics. Denver, Colorado: The Opicka Gallery, 10-31 May 1994. Brochure featured: *Hanging Houses of Cuenca, España*; *Inside Bab Smarin, Morocco*.

1995:

The Great American Landscape-A Fine Art Tribute. Cody, Wyoming: Big Horn Galleries Group. Traveling exhibition: Aspen, Colorado.

Plum Creek Cellars Exhibition. Denver, Colorado.

1996:

Travels with Buffalo. Denver, Colorado: Buffalo Kaplinski Gallery, 17-31 May 1996. Brochure featured: *Tiempo y Polvo*.

1997:

Mountains and Moors, Breckenridge, Colorado: Colorado Essence Galleries of Fine Art. Brochure featured: *Marten Creek, Above Leadville* (16" x 20"); *The Essence of Scotland/ Ben Nevis* (28" x 20").

1998:

The Colorists: Rick Stoner, Buffalo Kaplinski. Denver, Colorado: Merrill Gallery, 9-31 October 1998.

1999:

100 Years of the Art of Taos, Golden, Colorado. Foothills Art Center. The exhibition included works by Buffalo Kaplinski, Ken Bunn, George Carlson, Ned Jacob, Mark Daily, and Bill Sharer.
Emeritus Collection, Denver, Colorado: Channel 6 Art Auction.
Western Artists Exhibition. Trinidad, Colorado: Roy Mitchell Museum.

2000:

9th Governor's Invitational Art Show, Loveland, Colorado. Loveland Museum.

2001:

Santa Fe Trail Art Show. Santa Fe, New Mexico. Award: Best of Category (oil).
Los Angeles County Fair Wine Competition, Los Angeles, California. Award for Plum Creek Wine Label.
Palisade Wine Festival. Palisade, Colorado: poster artist.

2002:

Palisade Wine Festival. Palisade, Colorado: poster artist.

2003:

Taos Art Festival, Taos, New Mexico: Total Arts Gallery.
Group Art Show, Grand Junction, Colorado: Western Colorado Center for the Arts.
Dedication of Visitors Center, Red Rocks Park. Morrison, Colorado: Visitors Center, 15 December 2003, Commissioned painting: *A Masterpiece In Stone* (acrylic 48" x 60").

SELECTED BIBLIOGRAPHY

Ashton, Dore. *Picasso on Art: A Selection of Views.* New York: Viking Penguin, Inc. 1972. Reprinted in paperback: Da Capo Press, Inc., 1972. Page references are to paperback edition.

Barrett, Marjorie. *Rocky Mountain News* "Now" Sunday, 9 April 1978.

Bergreen, Lawrence. *Over the Edge of the World: Magellan's Terrifying Circumnavigation of the Globe.* New York, NY: Harper Collins Publishers, Inc., 2003.

Bickerstaff, Laura. *Pioneer Artists of Taos.* Rev. ed. Denver, Colorado: Old West Publishing Co., 1983.

Bouret, Jean. *The Barbizon School and the 19ᵗʰ Century French Landscape Painting.* Greenwich, CT: New York Graphic Society, Ltd., 1973.

Boyer, David. "Yosemite – Forever." *National Geographic,* January 1985.

Bradley, Jeff. "Foothills exhibition traces 100 years of Taos artistry." *Denver Post,* 31 January 1999.

Cameron, Ian. *Magellan and the First Circumnavigation of the World.* New York, NY: Saturday Review Press, 1973.

Chandler, Mary Voelz. *Guide to Denver Architecture with Regional Highlights.* Englewood, CO: Westcliffe Publishers, 2001.

Clark, Kenneth. *A Guide to Civilization: The Kenneth Clark Films on the Cultural Life of Western Man.* NY: Time-Life Films in association with the National Gallery of Art, 1970.

Dallas, Sandra. *Sacred Paint: Ned Jacob.* Santa Fe, NM: Fenn Galleries Publishing, Inc., 1979.

Danielsson, Bengt. *Gauguin in the South Seas.* Garden City, NY: Doubleday & Co., Inc., 1966.

Denver Post, 30 August 1970.

Gussow, Alan. *A Sense of Place: The Artist and the American Landscape.* San Francisco, CA: Friends of the Earth, Inc., 1972.

Harvey, Betty. "Buffalo Kaplinski." *Artists of the Rockies and Golden West,* September 1977.

Harvey, Eleonore. *The Voyage of the Icebergs: Frederic Church's Arctic Masterpiece.* New Haven, CT: Yale University Press in association with the Dallas Museum of Art, 2002.

Jellico, John. "The Infinite Landscapes of Buffalo Kaplinski." *American Artist,* August 1972.

Kinsey, Joni Louise. *Thomas Moran and the Surveying of the American West.* Washington, D.C.: Smithsonian Institution Press, 1992.

McKinney, Sam. *Bligh: A True Account of Mutiny aboard His Majesty's Ship Bounty.* Camden, ME: International Marine Publishing Co., 1989.

Miller, Marlan. "Galleries in Santa Fe, Taos Display Real Vigor." *Phoenix Gazette,* 30 August 1966.

Mills, James. "New Kaplinski Works Show His Exhilaration." *Denver Post,* 4 November 1979.

Price, Max. "Artist's Horizon Broadened." *Denver Post,* 13 October 1983.

"Kaplinski Turns to Painting of Ancient Cultures." *Denver Post,* 16 November 1984.

Ray, Diane. "The Greeley Art Scene." *Greeley (Colorado) Tribune,* 29 September 1976.

Richards, Bill. " The Untamed Yellowstone," *National Geographic,* August 1981.

"Artist Widens Subject Horizons." *Rocky Mountain News,* [ca. 13 October] 1983.

Romancito, Rick. "The Hard Bright Light of the West." *Taos News,* Tempo, 22 May 1997.

Scully, Vincent Joseph. *The Earth, The Temple, and the Gods: Greek Sacred Architecture.* New Haven, CT: Yale University Press, 1962.

Stewart, Rosemary. "Where Buffalo Roams." (Paper prepared for presentation at the Denver Fortnightly Club, Denver, Colorado, April 1995.)

Smart, Gene S. *American's Ancient Cities.* Washington, D.C.: National Geographic Society, 1988.

Traher, Frances. "Buffalo Kaplinski Side-stepping the Expected; Moving On." *Art West,* September 1984.

Wibberley, Leonard. *Fiji: Islands of the Dawn.* New York, NY: Ives Washburn, Inc., 1964.